Thriving in
Retirement

Thriving in Retirement

Lessons from Baby Boomer Women

Anne C. Coon and Judith Ann Feuerherm

Foreword by Mary Catherine Bateson

 PRAEGER™

An Imprint of ABC-CLIO, LLC
Santa Barbara, California • Denver, Colorado

Library of Congress Cataloging-in-Publication Data

Names: Coon, Anne Christine, author. | Feuerherm, Judith Ann, author.
Title: Thriving in retirement : lessons from baby boomer women/Anne C. Coon
    and Judith Ann Feuerherm ; foreword by Mary Catherine Bateson.
Description: Santa Barbara, California : Praeger, [2017] | Includes
    bibliographical references.
Identifiers: LCCN 2017024378 (print) | LCCN 2017036899 (ebook) |
    ISBN 9781440859977 (ebook) | ISBN 9781440859960 (alk. paper)
Subjects: LCSH: Women—Employment—United States. | Women—
    Retirement—United States. | Baby boom generation—United States.
Classification: LCC HD6095 (ebook) | LCC HD6095 .C72 2017 (print) |
    DDC 331.40973—dc23
LC record available at https://lccn.loc.gov/2017024378

ISBN: 978–1–4408–5996–0
EISBN: 978–1–4408–5997–7

21 20 19 18 17   1 2 3 4 5

This book is also available as an eBook.

Praeger
An Imprint of ABC-CLIO, LLC

ABC-CLIO, LLC
130 Cremona Drive, P.O. Box 1911
Santa Barbara, California 93116-1911
www.abc-clio.com

This book is printed on acid-free paper ∞

Manufactured in the United States of America

To Kurt Feuerherm and to Craig Zicari

Contents

Foreword *by Mary Catherine Bateson*   ix

Acknowledgments   xiii

Introduction   xvii

1 Baby Boomer Professional Women: Who Are They?   1

2 Family Influences   11

3 Building Careers in an Era of Change   31

4 At the Point of Transition: Individual Strengths and Concerns   55

5 The Confidence of a Cohort   77

6 "What's New?"   93

7 Why Are the Stories of Baby Boomer Women Important?   111

8 What Are the Lessons We Can All Take Away?   121

9 Postcareer but *Future*-Oriented   135

Afterword   145

Bibliography   153

Foreword

In the United States, in the course of the twenty-first century, one group after another came forward demanding fuller participation in the professions and in governance. The first of these movements was the Civil Rights Movement; the second, new wave feminism, followed by persons with disabilities and gay rights (now LGBTQ rights). We are currently in the process of working toward a new understanding of later adulthood to reap the benefit of increased longevity. In every one of these cases, the efforts of a marginalized group to achieve recognition have had broad implications for society.

In trying to describe the changes in women's lives, I have struggled to find metaphors that express the novelty and the achievement involved. When women were speaking of "juggling," an anxiety-producing metaphor, I suggested that they think of themselves as artists "composing" lives consisting of diverse and changing components. The process is *creative*. When men and women faced perplexity about "life after retirement," I emphasize that an artistic composition could involve balance and harmony of diverse components across time as well as in space and found myself emphasizing that increased longevity is not just an "add-on" but that, like a room added to a house, it leads to changes in the use of all the other rooms (or eras). And I added to the metaphor a life as a house of multiple rooms to live in, the metaphor of an "atrium": a central space with multiple doors in different directions, open to the sky, a new kind of freedom. Anne Coon and Judy Feuerherm have described that new and amazingly open room, through which the men and women of the Baby Boom are currently passing.

Some thirty years were added to life expectancy at birth in the twentieth century, primarily by scientific research and cultural changes. I believe that this change may prove to be as significant in human evolution as the extension of dependent childhood. The human pattern of survival is based not on fixed, inborn patterns of behavior, as in most of animal species, but on learning that can take very different forms and continues throughout the life course. It is this plasticity that has allowed humans to develop ways of living virtually everywhere on the planet and that offers hope that we will find the capacity for change that will be needed during the ecological and climatic disruption that lies ahead. Everywhere childhood seems to be getting longer, and lifelong learning is becoming a watchword, as it needs to be. Dependency is seen by many as a negative concept, but it is in the long period of childhood dependency that humans learn both love and trust and perhaps the courage to go forward into continuing change. I believe that interdependence and the empathy that supports cooperation are precisely what we need in our uncertain future.

What is most striking about the late adulthood choices made by these Boomer women is their movement into areas of change. They have found their careers in spaces created by twentieth-century feminism, and many of these are spaces that did not exist previously, new professions. Two striking examples are *coaching* (life or career coaching, not athletic coaching) and *museum curating* (such as caring for and making choices in museum collections). Other examples have to do with guiding technological change in the workplace and outplacement. The theme of "giving back" or making a contribution is also an important one.

Women seem to be becoming more thoughtful than men about what to do in later adulthood, for several reasons. Ageism is still more prevalent directed at women, so finding a role that is satisfying and effective is more challenging. More important, however, is the fact that women coming up on retirement today have already experienced a reassessment of their roles during the feminist movement: they have looked at what they might have taken for granted and recognized some of their assumptions as "internalized oppression," negative stereotypes to be put aside as they have claimed new freedom and new creativity. Furthermore, in many cases, having managed careers of multiple commitments, they are less narrowly focused than many men, more aware of the possible implications of decisions made for the wider human and ecological community. Because there is still a tendency for men to marry younger women, women maintain caregiving roles as wives and as grandparents longer than men. Add to this the fact that the need to adapt flexibly to moves forced by a husband's career changes may now be replaced by the need to adapt to moves to comfortable retirement sites where a wife's career shaped over many years may be interrupted. These factors mean that once again, as couples look toward their later years, women find themselves again looking within themselves and raising consciousness of their identities and goals. No wonder some find their way into life coaching and, indeed, into "curating" their own lives, for as one woman told the authors, "The wisdom part comes from choices." This is "active wisdom," associated not with a rocking chair but with moving forward.

These are women who were given little career guidance but were told that they could do whatever they set their minds on. Their choices are examples of creativity guided by common sense and the understanding that satisfaction comes from engagement. My advice to women reassessing their investment of themselves in later adulthood is biblical, for "where your treasure is (your time, talent, and skills), there will your heart be also." They are scouts entering a new landscape and modeling a sense of possibility to those who will follow—including the men in their lives.

Mary Catherine Bateson

Acknowledgments

FROM ANNE COON

We simply could not have written this book without the stories and insights of the women we have identified as "Cohort 25." The thoughtfulness, candor, and enthusiasm of these twenty-five women continually inspired us, and we are deeply grateful to each of them for their contributions to the book. We also appreciate the generosity with which they gave of their time to meet and talk with us on several occasions, to travel and attend focus group sessions, and to engage in follow-up conversations. They were active participants in a complex and recursive research process, and we thank each one of them for her commitment to this project.

A sincere thank-you as well to the editors who played a critical role in refining this manuscript, especially Hilary Claggett, of Praeger, ABC-CLIO, and Joanie Eppinga, of Eagle Eye Editing & Writing. Molly Q. Cort, of RIT Press, provided essential editorial and publishing advice, and the Authors Guild offered very helpful and timely guidance.

I am especially grateful for the early encouragement of Mary Catherine Bateson, whose work I have long admired, as well as the ongoing interest and support of many friends: Marcia Birken, Franlee Frank, Nicholas DiChario, Linda Garsin, Janet McOmber, Evelyn Brister, Kathy Vernam, Andrea Weinstein, Babak Elahi, and Sarah Collins. A special thank-you to Deborah Hughes for her thoughtful advice and introductions to interview subjects and to Diana Nyad for her enthusiastic support and inspiration.

As always, my husband, Craig Zicari, offered invaluable counsel and support from beginning to end of this project, and my daughter, Sarah Perlet, was a constant source of encouragement and inspiration.

Through our lengthy collaborative research and writing process, I learned an enormous amount from my coauthor, Judy Feuerherm. I came to better appreciate the importance of understanding a professional life within the context of the personal. Judy's ability to see the big picture, to recognize trends, and to design a solidly grounded research methodology allowed us to develop our initial questions into a multiyear, multitiered project.

A final word of appreciation to the Central Library of Rochester & Monroe County, a valuable resource in our community and a welcoming place for a writer.

FROM JUDY FEUERHERM

Our thanks to the many people who took the time to help us throughout the last few years as we developed this book, in particular, the members of Cohort 25 for their time, thinking, and responsiveness throughout this process; to Rebecca Rimel and Kim Parker of the Pew Charitable Trusts for their research assistance; to Bleu Cease at Rochester Contemporary Art Center (RoCo) for providing us space and the ease of setup for our first focus group and to former colleagues, Monica Morrow, Nancy Bevington, and Jayne Richards at Right Management, for their help and support during this project; to the New York City office administrative team for welcoming all of us and ensuring that the logistics and conference room setup met all our expectations; to Pauline Dimitry and Debby Mandt for recommending women for our study as well as Claire Brisset and Keith Talbot who also introduced us to members of our study and provided valuable thinking about our project; to Nadia Haridi for her thinking and sharing of best practices in our developing the focus groups; to Bill Borton, Claire Williams, and Kip Trum for taking the time to network us to their professional connections; and to Andy and John Ryan, Jim Tausch, Melissa Lord, and Lisa Weinert for their feedback and insights. A special thanks to Kerry Hannon for her introductions and her advice; to Janice Radway for her thinking, enthusiasm, and encouragement; to Julie Jansen for her generous time and discussion about her experiences in book publishing and marketing; and to Debra Englander for her communication and rapid response time in identifying a publisher that is a perfect fit for our book.

I am most grateful to my best friend and husband, Kurt Feuerherm, for his amazing support throughout these last four years; to my long-time friend, Chris Hutchinson, for her feedback and encouragement; to my nephew, Rob McConnell, for his thoughtful input; and finally, to my niece, Rhea Bowen, sister, Kathy McConnell, and friends Diane and Shelly Berlyn, Ray Demaio, Jan Kellner, Marie Tedeschi, Kristine Bouyoucos, and Lorraine and Marty Rosenbaum, for their support throughout this entire project.

I especially want to acknowledge and thank my coauthor, Anne Coon, for her amazing ability to weave together all the pieces of this project, from survey data to interview narratives and focus group discussions, and make them into a coherent, readable story that reflects the voices, knowledge, and lives of the women, who found, developed, and are now exiting their full-time careers only to establish, yet again, a new paradigm for retirement.

Introduction

"What's next?" If you are a professional woman in your late fifties to late sixties, you have certainly either asked or heard this question. Like you and thousands of other women, we also wondered what would come next after we left our full-time careers. Women of our generation vividly remember coming of age and getting our first jobs in a time when everything seemed to be changing. We seized opportunities, jumped in, and made our way, often entering fields previously dominated by men. We learned what we were capable of; we took risks and changed direction, and we grew. For decades now, we have played an active role in reshaping the workplace. Our opportunities, our drive, and our belief that we could take on anything have helped create a professional culture where the roles and expectations for women today are vastly different from what they were when we were growing up. We have also given extraordinary amounts of time, energy, and expertise to support, mentor, and expand opportunities for other women and girls.

As we move into retirement, our cohort of professional women is still carrying the values and innovative spirit that shaped our careers and reshaped the workplace. During our careers, we were changing at the same time our workplace was changing. We grew in experience and confidence and knew instinctively that we were becoming women who were very different from the women of our mothers' generation. Now, *what's next* can best be described as a continuation of that process. *What's next* is the opportunity for each of us to shape a new sense of identity. No longer defined by the professional positions we held, nor by expectations the generations before us may have had for life after age sixty, we are once again prepared to step forward and find out how our strengths, passions, and experiences will serve us in forging new, postcareer identities.

This book is in many ways a conversation among peers. As happens in conversations, questions are posed and answered; topics are raised and revisited. People tell stories. From the beginning, our intent was not to provide answers but to provide opportunities for women to talk to one another, to reflect on their lives and careers, and to make discoveries that were sometimes unique to each woman and sometimes shared by the group.

We will profile the women individually in Chapters 2 and 3 and quote frequently from their interviews and group conversations, but before we introduce the women and their stories, we believe it is important to introduce ourselves.

WHAT BROUGHT US TO THIS PROJECT?

Judy: It began over lunch. I had recently retired and began to realize that I was facing one of my most difficult transitions. I wanted to sort it out and think about what it meant and wondered who else was going through or anticipating this difficult phase. What were other women experiencing and how were they sorting it out? I asked my longtime friend, Anne, if she would like to talk about doing a project together. She agreed to meet, and we began a brainstorming phase that turned out to be the first step in this book. We each had different perspectives on how it could evolve and decided that it would make an interesting pairing of our professional backgrounds and interests.

My background is diverse, with common threads of problem solving, creativity, leadership, and coaching. I grew up in a privileged suburban town in an extended family after the death of my stepfather when I was seven years old. I excelled in school, and my mother instilled in me the idea that I could do anything I set my mind to. After high school, I began experimenting with who I was through education and hands-on work experience. I found I liked being on the edge: trying new things and moving on if they weren't a good fit. My career began in the corporate world, and then I made a decision to complete my undergraduate degree in art, which was followed by an art restoration business, a building restoration, and a fine art/antique gallery partnership. After three years, I decided to go back to school and get my master's degree in journalism in Philadelphia. Once I had completed the degree, a job offer at a local newspaper presented itself at the same time as an offer from an exciting real estate developer. I accepted the real estate development position, which rewarded me with a partnership. Through these job phases, my key skills emerged. After eight years and a financial market downturn, a new opportunity to develop a program for teaching marketing skills to nonprofit neighborhood development groups in Washington, DC, was presented to me, and I accepted. After a year, I became fascinated with, and decided to see if I could use my skills in, the corporate career transition area. I had nothing to lose. I interviewed and accepted a job in the New York City area, and a career evolved that lasted twenty years.

Most important, and most critical to this project, were the last fifteen to twenty years of my career, in which I developed strong coaching expertise with a focus on the executive level and C-Suite. I learned by listening carefully, paying attention to people, and then probing to understand the dimensions of what they were saying and not saying. I began to appreciate the fact that individuals make the best decisions for themselves if they have a process to follow that looks at and evaluates their personal and career histories so they can more clearly think about and prioritize their next steps. Often, a group format combined with individual coaching provides a rich context for individuals to broaden their thinking. The biggest reward in the coaching process is when you act as a catalyst, allowing individuals to assimilate information and make their own decisions, which sometimes surprise them as well as you! This project has helped me focus and be more reflective on my personal transition. The women in this study have been open and honest, and it has been very exciting to work with them.

Anne: Like many of the women we met through our research, I, too, *loved* school as a child. From a very early age, I was curious about the world beyond my rural hometown. My passion for reading fed this curiosity, and along with the encouragement of a few teachers, it helped me imagine a future as a writer or a teacher. Eventually, I made a career of both. When I entered college at a large state university, I was exhilarated by the challenge of making my way in a brand-new environment. An early marriage and divorce while still in my twenties left me more committed than ever to having a career. As a single mother, I took on multiple adjunct teaching positions, freelance writing, and tutoring, all the while knowing it was imperative that I finish my doctorate. When I was offered a full-time position in the learning skills center of a large, technological university, I accepted, and I set a goal for myself to either complete my PhD or make the decision to abandon it by the time I turned thirty-five. Teaching full-time, studying and writing at night and on weekends, I went back, completed my qualifying exams, and wrote my dissertation. With PhD in hand, at thirty-four, I went on to become a tenured professor of English and accepted several administrative appointments, including university-wide director of writing and senior associate dean in the College of Liberal Arts.

Much of my early professional writing arose from the literature I was teaching as well as the teaching itself, but I was especially open to and excited by unexpected writing projects. The first of these came when I was invited to edit the unpublished speeches of Amelia Bloomer, an early women's rights reformer. I read hundreds of hand-written pages of Bloomer's prose, became accustomed to her voice, and chronicled her emerging identity as a public speaker.

An experimental teaching assignment, in which I was asked to develop a critical thinking course with a mathematician, evolved into a unique, long-term teaching and writing collaboration on the intersections of mathematics and poetry. This work was cited in national publications and conferences and was celebrated by the university. The experience of integrating my literature background with critical inquiry in another field drove my interest in creativity across the disciplines, and I began to seek out creative partnerships with artists, engineers, and musicians.

My writing and publishing history is marked by an openness to new ideas, a long-standing interest in the voices and insights of others, and a curiosity about how individuals' work and identity are intertwined. All of these qualities prepared me in different ways for this project. When Judy and I first talked about interviewing professional Baby Boomer women, I was intrigued by the opportunity for discovery. I wanted to hear what women had to say and see how their stories might speak to and speak for other women. What had they experienced? What had they learned? What insights were they carrying with them now?

Bringing women's words together, giving them shape, and looking for patterns has been a challenging and extremely gratifying process. Women confided in us, shared their thoughts with one another, and, both individually and collectively, arrived at important insights. As a researcher and writer, I am grateful for the women's generosity and candor. As a peer, a Baby Boomer whose career has been marked by changes in direction and leaps into the unknown, I am happy to be a part of this cohort of women.

Now making my own transition from full-time teaching and administration to focus on writing, I am benefiting from what I have learned about the acceptance and confidence that come from listening to our stories and sharing them with others. Stories give us an invaluable way of understanding our experience and passing on what we have learned and struggled with. The language we use reflects our self-awareness, how we see ourselves, and how we respond to opportunity, challenges, and change.

WHO ARE THE WOMEN WE STUDIED?

To identify participants for this study, we began by reaching out to our respective networks of professional women. Our initial contacts soon led to an expanding group of referrals that included women from a range of backgrounds and professions. We chose to look exclusively at career women—that is, individuals committed to the long-term professional engagement and growth demanded by their field(s). Our first group of interview subjects came from western New York State. The second group was drawn from the metropolitan areas of New York, New Jersey, Massachusetts, and Pennsylvania.

The twenty-five women profiled in this book represented a range of ethnic and geographic backgrounds, areas of professional focus, and current employment status as well as diversity in race, sexual orientation, and marital status. We are committed to presenting their individual responses as accurately as possible while respecting their privacy and adhering to our guarantee of confidentiality. To ensure this, we refer to each woman by a pseudonym, and we have aggregated all demographic information. The views of women in the focus groups are brought together collectively to represent the consensus that emerged within the groups.

DRAWING ON COACHING STRATEGIES, LISTENING TO STORIES

As much as possible, we wanted to make women's stories personal, to capture their voices and use their own language. We also wanted to understand those stories within the larger context of the early Baby Boomer generation. What were the women's experiences as children, young adults, and professionals? What distinguished the women from one another? What did they have in common?

To develop a personalized, recursive approach, we drew on the coaching process Judy had used professionally and then incorporated and modified several components into the basis of our work. In place of an oral life history, we created a six-page survey. The survey posed in-depth questions about women's early influences from childhood to adulthood, including their relationships with parents, family, friends, and mentors, followed by questions about their educational choices, expectations, and career path. The survey also asked about their decision to stay in or leave the workplace and their ideas about their next steps. In addition to providing valuable demographic data, the survey helped us identify important similarities and differences among the women, both as they were growing up and in their professional lives.

After women completed the survey, we used coaching strategies in lieu of assessment tools to communicate with them directly and to develop an awareness of their thinking and behavioral styles.[1] Based on each woman's survey responses, we then developed questions for an individualized sixty-minute interview; during the interview, we asked each participant to elaborate on and clarify her responses. Whether conducted by phone or in person, the interviews gave us an opportunity to interact directly with the women. We listened to their stories, told in their own voices. We learned about the roadblocks and opportunities they experienced; the hard work and years they invested; and the credentials and recognition they earned. At the time of the interviews, the women were at various points along a continuum that included a search for work, part-time and full-time employment, and retirement. To learn more about each person's transition to life beyond her full-time career, we asked questions that focused on timing and other factors affecting the decision to retire.

Although the questions we posed in surveys and personal interviews told us a great deal about the lives and decisions of individual women, we realized how important it was for them to talk to others like themselves. We created that opportunity in the next phase of our research when we brought the women together. After interviewing a dozen women in each of the two geographic areas, we invited each set of participants to be part of a focus group. Their responses were very enthusiastic.

We convened the groups for morning-long sessions to gather and assimilate more in-depth group information.[2] The focus group discussions gave women the opportunity to engage in a process of self-reflection that continued long after the meetings had concluded. For many women, the focus group conversation and shared experiences sparked the beginning of a new kind of self-awareness.

In addition to providing us with valuable information about the women's shared experiences and concerns, the focus groups played a critical role in developing the element of reciprocity that we believe is vital to our work. We wanted the participants to walk away feeling uplifted, with a better understanding of the transition process they were going through. We wanted them to know they had been heard, to feel they had shared their own experiences and benefited from those of other women.

The element of reciprocity also had a role in stimulating women's thinking. Many women commented that completing the survey gave them the opportunity to think about their lives and careers in a way they never had. Their interviews encouraged even greater self-reflection, and they came to the focus groups ready to share their thoughts with one another.

Our research culminated with follow-up telephone interviews conducted one year after the initial in-depth interviews. In these calls, we posed simple, straightforward questions, asking women about any insights they had experienced during the intervening months. As we will see in Chapter 6, these open-ended questions produced a surprising similarity of answers addressing identity, physical space, and friendship.[3]

STORIES THAT NEED TO BE CHRONICLED

When we began, we had no idea what women would reveal or how much the individual accounts of their careers would overlap with one another. What we discovered was that women had an overwhelming desire to talk and connect with others. We also discovered that during their careers, regardless of location or profession, they had remarkably similar experiences. As we listened and learned from them, our hypothesis that Baby Boomer professional women, as a cohort, had important things to say and professional lives and stories that needed to be chronicled was affirmed.

The women we met all had stories about their careers—moments of personal triumph, of breaking a barrier, of receiving advice that went against the norm. They also had stories of defeat—losing a job, being passed over, or being told their ideas would never fly. They entered kindergarten between 1951 and 1961, the years when America was booming with postwar growth. Most of them were raised with the expectation that they would marry and have children. Many of them had fathers or mothers, sometimes both, who encouraged them without reservation. Some had mothers who worked outside their home. Almost all said they had little or no career guidance in high school or college, but they loved school and were competitive academically. Many of the women also found ways to compete athletically, even though Title IX of the Education Amendments, the comprehensive federal law prohibiting discrimination on the basis of sex in any federally funded education program or activity, was not passed until

1972, two years before the last of this cohort graduated from high school.

Many of our subjects said they initially pursued a career because they "needed to earn a living," before they knew what they wanted to do professionally. Yet regardless of where they started, they completed the formal training and advanced degrees required for a variety of professions. For thirty or more years, the women in this group dealt with the complexities of building and advancing their careers while juggling personal commitments and relationships. Discrimination in the workplace was part of the culture in many work settings, and several women described experiencing unwanted sexual advances, dealing with innuendo, being paid less than men, and being denied opportunities for advancement because of gender or race. Others started their own companies from the ground up, figuring things out and finding allies as they went along. In general, the women took charge in their lives, professionally and personally. They had few, if any, role models, but most of them recalled one or two individuals—sometimes a professor or a supervisor—who offered critically important inspiration, advice, or support.

Once again, the women were taking charge as they made the transition to lives beyond their full-time careers. They were challenged to redefine themselves and identify their passions. Without the structures, opportunities, and rewards that shaped their careers, the path going forward was less clear and more individualized. Despite what they shared as a cohort, each woman was discovering that she had to find her own way to focus her energies and go on with her story.

LESSONS FOR A GENERATION

We have learned that concerns about the next steps after retirement are not a small or isolated issue. Many people—women and men—have expressed an interest in our research and how it might apply to them. Based upon what we have learned from the women themselves, we have developed a chapter of lessons for a broader audience. Although Baby Boomer women professionals will certainly be able to make connections to their own experiences, we are confident that Baby Boomer men, too, as well as younger women and men will discover in the women's lessons words of advice and encouragement and a new way of thinking about the years after their full-time careers.

We took the opportunity in the Afterword to reflect deliberately on the use of the word "retirement" and its related forms. The word has a significant place at the heart of our work, but for the women in

Cohort 25, it simply didn't seem like an accurate description for what they were experiencing or how they saw their future. Recognizing that many thoughtful attempts have been made to come up with an alternative way of referring to the years after a full-time career, we have taken the view that it is more important to focus on how these Baby Boomer professional women were *actually living in and changing* the period of life that had historically been referred to as retirement. Just as their generation changed the expectations and environment of the workplace, they were again poised to make a dramatic change and leave their mark as the largest group of women ever to move on from professional careers. Strengthened by personal experience, professional expertise, and good health, they were ready to model a new kind of life going forward.

INTRODUCING COHORT 25

As our group of subjects took shape and we learned more about them, we knew we had identified a good team! They were a strong, diverse, and balanced group that we think represents well the First Wave of Baby Boomer women professionals. They were, by virtue of their education and careers, women who had enjoyed many kinds of privilege. Some had also experienced poverty, very difficult personal challenges, and discrimination. When they met one another, they easily acknowledged the similarities in their experiences, just as they valued and were curious about one another's individual stories. We are confident that their experiences provide insights into those in the larger group of their Baby Boomer peers.

In writing about the women, we encountered an editorial challenge that we solved by coining the term "Cohort 25." Rather than repeatedly referring to "the women in the group" or "the women here," we decided to create a name we could use when we refer collectively to our research participants. We felt the name should reflect the sense of camaraderie and shared identity that emerged among the women. Thus, we created "Cohort 25" as a collective designation for the twenty-five women who lent their stories and wisdom to this book.

We believe *Thriving in Retirement* will generate a complex, peer-to-peer conversation among Baby Boomer women professionals. Women will find experiences similar to their own and will identify with the challenges and successes of the women of Cohort 25. At the same time, they will take heart and be encouraged by the resourcefulness and reflections of others. We believe the book will encourage women to take a long look at their own careers, listen carefully to the stories they tell, and embrace the strengths and passions that are already preparing them for their next steps.

NOTES

1. Through years of coaching individuals incorporating the use of assessment tools such as the Myers-Briggs Type Indicator (MBTI) and the Life Styles Inventory (LSI), Judy gained an awareness of how personalities are revealed in individuals' career choices, language, and approaches to people and problem solving.

2. Each group ranked and then responded to a list of topics we had identified from the surveys and interviews. To ensure that the topics accurately reflected the concerns of the group, we invited the women to add any topics they felt were overlooked and delete any they felt were not relevant. Each group was then divided into two subgroups that worked independently before coming back together to present feedback and engage in further discussion. We stayed off to the side during this process, taking our own notes and acting as observers.

3. The timeline of our research was as follows:Following each woman's completion of the survey, we conducted personal interviews by telephone or in person between April 1, 2014, and December 11, 2014. We held focus group meetings in Rochester, New York, on October 22, 2014, and in New York City on January 14, 2015, and conducted follow-up telephone calls in December 2015.

1

Baby Boomer Professional Women: Who Are They?

Although the label "Baby Boomers" refers collectively to seventy-six million postwar children born primarily in the United States between 1946 and 1964, the nineteen-year cohort is often broken into two groups. The professional women whose words and experiences make up this book are members of what is commonly considered the First Wave of Baby Boomers, individuals born between 1946 and 1956.[1] Most, but not all, were children whose fathers were returning to civilian life after military service and whose mothers, often after holding wartime jobs, were returning to the home, focused on becoming homemakers. The First Wave or early Baby Boomers can be distinguished from their younger brothers and sisters (Second Wave or late Baby Boomers) in many ways, but for purposes of exploring the influences that shaped their personal and professional lives, the defining or key events during the period in which they reached young adulthood are critical. In analyzing birth cohorts, Reynolds Farley identifies the Civil Rights Movement and the Sexual Revolution as key events at the time early Baby Boomers reached young adulthood, while for the later Boomers, the era of employment restructuring of the mid-1970s through the 1980s is viewed as the key event of the time.[2] Not surprisingly, for the parents of Baby Boomers (born between 1916 and 1935), Farley points to World War II and the postwar boom as key events at the time they became young adults. The radiating effects of these defining events, whether they involve significant social change or the destruction of war, certainly influence an entire family, from grandparents to infants, but when the events occur during the years when young people are just coming of age, they exert an influence and create expectations that can shape a career and last a lifetime.

The Baby Boomers began entering kindergarten in 1951. By the time they were teenagers, the women interviewed for this book—early Baby Boomer girls who went on to have careers—were living in a world where opportunity and turbulence were colliding, a world that appeared full of possibility. Many were explicitly told by their parents that with hard work and good education, they could "do anything." Even though legal restrictions still posed barriers to access and opportunity, those barriers were beginning to fall away, almost at the very moment these young women were coming of age.

FIRST WAVE BABY BOOMERS: A SNAPSHOT OF THEIR FIRST THIRTY YEARS

1946–56	**First Wave Baby Boomers born.**
1951–61	**First Wave Baby Boomers enter kindergarten.**
1955	Rosa Parks refuses to give up her seat to a white man on a bus in Montgomery, Alabama.
1960	Food and Drug Administration approves birth control pills. Wilma Rudolph becomes the first American woman to win three gold medals in track and field at a single Olympics.
1961	John F. Kennedy establishes the Presidential Commission on the Status of Women. The commission's final report (1963) recommends affordable child care, equal employment opportunities for women, and paid maternity leave.
1963	Betty Friedan publishes *The Feminine Mystique*. The Equal Pay Act makes it illegal for employers to pay women less than men for the same job. Reverend Martin Luther King Jr. delivers his "I Have a Dream" speech on the steps of the Lincoln Memorial.
1964–74	**First Wave Baby Boomers graduate from high school and enter college. They have grown up with the mantra, "With education, you can accomplish whatever you want."**
1964	Title VII of the Civil Rights Act and Equal Employment Opportunity Commission bars discrimination in employment based on race and sex.
1965	The Supreme Court strikes down a law prohibiting the use of contraceptives by married couples.
1966	NOW (National Organization of Women) is founded.
1967	The affirmative action policy of 1965 is expanded to cover sex-based discrimination.

1968–78	**First Wave Baby Boomers graduate from college and begin entering the workforce.**
1968	The rock musical *Hair* opens on Broadway.
	The Equal Employment Opportunity Commission rules that male/female segregated "help wanted" ads in newspapers are illegal.
1969	The Stonewall Riots become a defining moment in the movement for lesbian, gay, bisexual, and transgender (LGBT) rights.
1971	The Twenty-Sixth Amendment to the U.S. Constitution lowers the voting age from twenty-one to eighteen.
	Ms. Magazine is published.
1972	The Supreme Court rules that an unmarried person has the right to use contraceptives.
	Title IX bans discrimination based on sex in education programs or activities provided by schools receiving federal financial assistance.
	Marlo Thomas releases her children's record *Free to Be ... You and Me*.
	Helen Reddy's song "I Am Woman" is released as a single and eventually sells over a million copies.
1973	The Boston Women's Health Book Collective publishes *Our Bodies, Ourselves*.
	Billie Jean King triumphs over Bobby Riggs in the "Battle of the Sexes" tennis match.
	The Supreme Court establishes a woman's right to abortion.
1974	Equal Credit Opportunity Act prohibits discrimination in consumer credit practices on the basis of sex, race, color, marital status, religion, national origin, age, or receipt of public assistance.
	The Supreme Court rules that employers cannot justify paying women lower rates than men for the same job strictly on the basis of their sex.
1976–86	**First Wave Baby Boomers turn thirty years old.**
1978	The Pregnancy Discrimination Act prohibits sex discrimination on the basis of pregnancy, so a woman cannot be fired or denied a job or promotion because she is or may become pregnant.
1983	Sally Ride becomes the first American woman to fly in space.

(continued)

| 1984 | Geraldine Ferraro is the first female vice presidential candidate representing a major American political party. The city of Berkeley, California, becomes the first city to offer its employees domestic-partnership benefits. |
| 1986 | Oprah Winfrey launches *The Oprah Winfrey Show.* |

In the popular culture, a dramatic evolution was taking place in attitudes toward women's rights and opportunities. Television, movies, books, and magazines made it clear to young women that things were changing. And those changes had real impact as women entered college and took their first jobs. Whether emboldened or just curious about what was out there, they were about to discover what the new social and legal environment would mean for them personally. They were prepared to find their place in society and were looking for ways to prove themselves.

When we met them, the women of Cohort 25 were looking back and realizing they had spent their lives figuring things out. From the beginning, they had been confident and resourceful, qualities that had given them momentum and driven their careers. They were undeterred when history or precedent, the rules or people around them, said *no*. Instead of abandoning their professional goals or losing focus under the demands of balancing a career and a family, they pressed on. They found ways to make things work. Sometimes, they drew on the support and encouragement of their family members or peers. Other times, they truly felt they were on their own.

As was the case throughout their careers, professional women Baby Boomers were not actively looking for role models or mentors at the point when they were leaving their full-time careers. They acknowledged the impact certain individuals had on them—both women and men—but the women always knew they needed to rely upon themselves as they moved forward professionally, often in areas women had not entered before. From early on, many of them were the "firsts." One woman in our study was the first girl in her town to have a newspaper route. Between years of college, another was the first woman to drive a mail truck in her community. Another was the first pregnant medical resident in her hospital. They told these stories with pride and humor. In some cases, being the first was sheer happenstance; sometimes, it meant raising some eyebrows, and in other cases, being the first posed serious challenges to the status quo and became the impetus for lasting change. Many of these women were at the center of changes that reshaped the culture or policies of an organization.

Their early achievements, whether small or grand in scale, whether personal or public, positioned women for years of hard work, confidence, and professional growth. Time after time, they moved into situations where they knew they had to break new ground. They knew they were competent, and they knew they had what it would take to be successful. Women of Cohort 25 often turned to language reminiscent of frontier days when they described what it took to persevere. "We had spunk" or "I had gumption," they said. This assertive language allowed women to place their career accomplishments in a larger context, to align themselves, perhaps unwittingly, with pioneers and heroes of another era. This language also conveyed another quality we often observed in the women: their optimism. They were not people who dwelt on disappointments or defeats. Even when thinking about the challenges or roadblocks they encountered in their careers, they were most often upbeat, funny, and self-reflective in a very positive way. These traits continued to serve them well as they looked forward to what would come next.

DEMOGRAPHICS

One of our primary commitments in writing this book is to present the stories of a diverse group of women. (See Table 1.1: Profiles.) We are confident that the careers and lives of the women of Cohort 25 will resonate with countless other professional Baby Boomer women. Certainly, each woman's life, both professional and personal, was uniquely her own, but the shared experiences of this generation, the stories of careers undertaken within an exceptional historical period, were fascinating and instructive. The women of Cohort 25 presented us with insights and questions that will be of interest to others, across generations, professions, and geographical boundaries. We will introduce them individually in Chapters 2 and 3, but here is a snapshot of who they were as a group.

All of the women we interviewed were born between 1946 and 1956, and at the time of their interviews, all of them spent at least part of the year in the northeastern United States; collectively, however, they had lived and/or worked in sixteen states and eight countries outside the United States. The women represented diversity in profession, background, race, ethnicity, marital status, and sexual preference. Some grew up in northern industrial cities, some in the Deep South, and others in the midwestern United States and Europe. Their families lived in urban centers and suburban developments, on farms, and on college campuses. Their fathers' work experiences were just as far-ranging as the Baby Boomer daughters' careers turned out to be. Some fathers worked for corporations, and others were employed in educa-tion, law, government, health care, and the military. Many were self-employed, owning businesses or family farms. Some of the women's fathers died at a young age, leaving their wives to raise families alone.

The mothers of our subjects represented a range of experiences sim-ilar to those of many other wives and mothers of the 1950–60s. Some were college-educated, with careers in teaching or nursing. Some worked full-time for the government or were active partners in a fam-ily business. Others were homemakers, often involved in community or religious organizations.

As women talked about their parents, they often spoke of factors that shaped the culture and values of their families. The shaping influ-ence of a family-owned business, a father's military career, or a tradi-tion of teaching and service imparted a powerful sense of cohesiveness to some families. In other cases, where a woman's parents were refugees or Holocaust survivors, their history of dis-placement and suffering was integral to the family's identity and deci-sions. Strong religious or ethnic identities also influenced the values in several families.

Looking at their earned degrees, areas of career experience, and years of professional employment, we see a group of women charac-terized by high achievement and professional commitment. As we learned from their interviews, many of the women in Cohort 25 changed direction or pursued additional degrees as their career goals evolved; collectively, the group of twenty-five earned twenty-nine degrees beyond the baccalaureate, including MA, MS, MFA, MBA, PhD, EdD, JD, and MD.

The average number of years of professional employment for the women was 35.8 years. Some women entered and remained in one profession for their entire career, while others made strategic moves, starting their own businesses or perhaps being recruited to take posi-tions in different fields or international organizations. Several began their careers as teachers, although many moved into other areas. Over half of the women worked in for-profit corporations or were self-employed at some point. Over a third were employed in the nonprofit corporate sector, higher education teaching and administration, or pri-vately owned companies. Other areas representing the range of the women's careers were government, health care, law, business partner-ships, performing and fine arts, coaching, and counseling.

When we turn to their personal lives, we find that at the time of their interviews, the majority of the women were married. The majority also had children, and very often, they had raised their children at the same time that they were pursuing their careers. Some took time off to stay at home with young children, but many did not. They balanced home and family and worked out childcare and school arrangements. Although the average number of children in the general population of Baby Boomer women born between 1946 and 1964 is 2.4, the average number of children for the eighteen mothers in the group was 1.88.

As we will see, the women in Cohort 25 were directly affected by changes in society. Here, briefly, are some of the critical changes that were taking place as they grew up and began their careers. Their stories demonstrate the impact these large-scale changes had on their individual lives.

CHANGES IN THE FAMILY

The aftermath of World War II had opened new education and employment opportunities for men in the United States, while in general, women were focused on raising families and being homemakers. Even if they were not in the workforce, women who were educated benefited financially. Often, one particular benefit was that they married college-educated men with high earning potential.[3] This was the milieu of opportunity in which the parents of Baby Boomers raised their children. They encouraged their sons to secure good educations and careers in order to support wives and families; daughters were told they could do anything they set their minds to, and education ensured them a backup plan if they needed to earn a living.

Changes that took place in the years between 1960 and 1973 (when the women of Cohort 25 were between the ages four and twenty-seven) dramatically affected women's personal lives. The introduction of the birth control pill, no-fault divorce, unmarried persons' right to use contraceptives, women's right to abortion, and women's ability to have their own credit cards were changes that had a very real impact on women's lives. Publications such as *The Feminine Mystique* (1963) and *Ms. Magazine* (1971) brought women's issues directly into the public eye and helped redefine society's views on marriage, divorce, sexual behavior, and women's roles in the home and the workplace.

CHANGES IN THE WORKPLACE

While there certainly were women who pursued successful careers in the generations that preceded them, Baby Boomer women entered the workforce at one of the most significant periods of change in the

Table 1.1 Profiles

Number of women in the study	Twenty-five
Years born	Sixteen women from 1946 through 1949 Nine women from 1951 through 1955
Areas of diversity	Profession Background Ethnicity Marital status Sexual preference
Where they grew up	Urban centers and suburban developments, on farms and college campuses
Degrees	Twenty-nine degrees beyond a bachelor's degree: 76% MA, MS 12% MFA, MBA 12% PhD and EdD 12% JD 4% MD
Average years of employment	35.8
Locations where women lived or worked	Sixteen states across the United States but primarily in the Northeast Eight countries outside of the United States, in Europe, Asia, the Middle East, and Africa
Range of career areas	Government Legal Business partnerships Entrepreneurship Performing and fine arts Coaching and counseling Education, K–12 and higher education Health care
Current marital status	Seventeen married Eight divorced, single, or widowed
Children	Eighteen, with an average of 1.88 per person
Grandchildren	56% said no and 44% said yes

nation's history. Beginning in the 1960s, changes arising from the Civil Rights Movement and antidiscrimination laws opened new doors of possibility for women and had a profound influence on how Americans thought and acted in the public arena.

The Civil Rights Act of 1964 had enormous significance for women as well as blacks. This act was hard won by powerful black leaders of the 1960s to ensure that their voting rights were protected and that racial discrimination was banned in the workplace and public places. In what has been seen by some as an attempt to quash the Civil Rights Act, Congressman Howard Smith, a longtime segregationist, amended the language to include sex as a discriminating characteristic. Smith's motives were not entirely clear since the Equal Pay Act of 1963 had already been passed, making it illegal to pay women less than men for the same job, and opposition to discrimination on the basis of sex had been gaining momentum.[4] Regardless of his motives, Smith's action resulted in protection from employment discrimination on the basis of sex being added to the Civil Rights Act and passed into law in 1964. This was followed by changes in state laws that had previously limited women's hours and type of work.[5]

In 1964, the women of Cohort 25 were between the ages eight and eighteen. The changes created by the Civil Rights Act meant that protections in the workplace expanded at the very time when they might have been looking for their first jobs. At the same time, the encouragement of their families—who told them throughout their childhoods that they could do anything they put their minds to—had produced a generation of women uniquely prepared to enter a changing workplace.

Their stories will tell us much more.

NOTES

1. Although the demarcation of birth years between First and Second Wave Baby Boomers is variously set at 1955 or 1956, for the purposes of our research, we have used the decade 1946–56 as the birth years of the cohort we are studying.

2. "Information about Birth Cohorts," Table 2-1. Reynolds Farley, *The New American Reality: Who We Are, How We Got Here, Where We Are Going* (New York: Russell Sage Foundation, 1996), 25.

3. Farley, *The New American Reality*, 5.

4. "The Civil Rights Act of 1964: A Long Struggle for Freedom," Library of Congress, accessed March 28, 2017, https://www.loc.gov/exhibits/civil-rights-act/epilogue.html.

5. Once the laws were in place, they were both implemented and challenged. As Baby Boomer women charged forward, they were asserting their role in history. A landmark example is the AT&T discrimination suit filed in the 1970s. Hearings showed that women workers had been excluded from any job above low-paying clerical and phone operators. AT&T settled out of court, paying fifteen million dollars in back wages plus twenty-three million dollars in raises to thirty-six thousand employees to compensate for pay discrimination based on previous policies. They agreed to implement effective, affirmative action programs. This case (settled in 1973) set a precedent and put "teeth" in the Civil Rights Act. For more on the AT&T decision, see Lois Kathryn Herr, *Women, Power, and AT&T* (Northeastern University Press, 2003), 152.

2

Family Influences

The First Wave of Baby Boomer women turned eighteen between the years of 1964 and 1974. They entered college and took their first jobs in a period of growing opportunity and freedom. Their parents' generation had offered role models for hard work and getting ahead, and the gender roles for men and women had been clearly defined. But American culture was undergoing enormous changes, from the schisms created by the Vietnam War to the sexual freedom offered by the Pill and the popular appeal of music, films, and fashions directed toward the young. The world opening up before an eighteen-year-old woman was vastly different from that experienced by her mother a generation earlier. What were the influences on this generation of young women? Who and what did they want to become? What factors led some of them to follow paths that would lead to professional careers? (See Table 2.1: Family Backgrounds and Choosing Careers.)

In response to the question, "Was it implicitly understood that you would go to college?" most of the women in Cohort 25 answered yes. From more detailed questions about their family background and the influences on their career direction, a complex portrait emerges, revealing many of the factors—in family, schools, and the broader culture—that shaped this cohort of girls.

PARENTS AND FAMILY DYNAMICS

"Did your mother work/have a career?" The number of mothers who worked full-time was slightly higher than that of those who did not work at all. Of the mothers who worked full-time, three were teachers and two worked with their husbands in farming. Other full-time positions held by the women's mothers included college professor, teletype setter, switchboard operator, librarian, and department supervisor for the federal government.

Some mothers were widowed at a young age; others were intermittently left in charge of their home for extended periods of time during their husbands' absence. When their husbands returned, the women resumed their roles as homemakers. The opportunities available to some women were strictly controlled by their husbands. No matter what their mothers' roles in the family were, daughters learned lessons in juggling responsibilities and in making accommodations.

In response to the question, "Was your mother influential in your career decision?" the majority of the women answered yes. Sometimes, a mother's influence was indirect or oblique, as these women described: "Indirectly ... she was a teacher, and I was a teacher ... but more important, I was exposed early on to museums and art and while I was not encouraged to pursue a career in museums and the arts, I certainly had my interest and enthusiasm in that domain kindled by my mother" and "My mother wanted me to be a teacher but allowed me to choose my college major. Ultimately, I wound up working at the university, but I have never been a teacher."

There were also instances when a mother's influence resulted from tragedy, as in the case of the daughter who, from an early age, understood the lasting impact of her mother's suffering in the Holocaust. Her daughter's desire to help others led to a career in psychoanalysis.

The influence of their mothers was very different for Elizabeth and Flora:

> She encouraged me to learn about art.
>
> Elizabeth, *artist/interior designer*

When Elizabeth was bullied as a girl, her mother encouraged her to "love the unloving" and took her to a gallery to help her learn about art. Her father traveled internationally for his company and was gone for extended periods, during which her mother took charge of the household and family until his return. Elizabeth's father assumed she would go on and get a teaching degree, and she did, but his focus was primarily on her brother's education and career development. Elizabeth's interest in art grew, and though her mother was adamant that she have a career and something other than her art to fall back on, she chose her college because of its bronze foundry. In that college, the head of the art department was a strong promoter of women. He encouraged Elizabeth to study sculpture in San Miguel de Allende, Mexico, and she did so several times. After college, Elizabeth taught elementary and secondary art in Ohio before moving with her husband to New York City. There, she worked as a designer at Bloomingdale's and began an interior design business. After relocating to western New York State, she taught design at the college level and began working with a prominent interior designer, where she continued for more than thirty years. At the time of her interview, she considered it a luxury to have been able to work for herself and still have time for her family and her volunteer work. She acknowledged that it was very hard to let go of her career. Although she looked forward to returning to sculpture again in retirement, she had questions about her identity and purpose. She asked, "How do I think of myself? What am I doing of value? Will other people see me differently?"

My mother said, "Teaching is a wonderful career."

Flora, *teacher specializing in K–5 special education and curriculum design*

Although Flora's mother did not go to college, she thought teaching was "the best thing ever." She set up a blackboard and desk in the basement of their home and "programmed" Flora at a young age to be a teacher. Her father died when Flora was twelve, and she later realized, "Maybe he would have been more of an influence as I matured." Flora did go on to earn a degree in education but was bored and ready to give up teaching after her maternity leave. Pennsylvania's then newly mandated gifted education program provided an opportunity for the stimulation and creativity she craved. She switched to K–5 gifted education, and after that, there was always something new with her job each year. She especially enjoyed writing creative cross-disciplinary curriculum and implementing it with students. As she said, "I never wanted to retire." Yet by the end of her career, she felt the field of education had changed drastically, and she was "walking through the days without the enthusiasm I once had." After working for forty years, except for the period when she was on maternity leave, in retirement she woke up every day and felt as though she was on vacation. What she loved best was not having structure in her life, but she remained very active. She was involved in a successful philanthropic endeavor in which she worked with other women to select and fund community projects each year. Flora liked this model of collective giving and was very pleased by the process and outcomes of the group's decisions. From spending quality time with her grandchildren to getting together with a friend she had known since graduate school, as well as teaching and playing Canasta, Flora was deeply engaged with her family, friends, and community. Despite her many active roles, she was looking for more: "I think older people can be very valuable in the work force on some level. I think there are many women like me who would like to do something, but don't know what. I still have a lot in me."

Although many mothers encouraged their daughters to pursue traditional careers, sometimes maternal encouragement was broad and unconditional. As one woman said, "She always talked about it being important for me to have a career. She said I could do anything I wanted—gave me confidence and a wide view of possibilities."

When a mother's advice combined nontraditional possibilities with a practical edge, the results could be quite inspiring, sending the daughter in a direction very different from that of her mother.

One mother was a part-time bookkeeper; her daughter became an attorney:

> She did not torture me after graduating from college to start a career right away, although she did think I ought to pursue an opportunity with the U.S. government that presented itself to me a year or so later ... She felt strongly that I should have a credentialed profession and thought being a lawyer would give me independence and financial security that could last a lifetime ... She trained me to be careful, detail-oriented in my work; gave me an appreciation for having my own money so I could spend it and have security; gave me the hard skills of bookkeeping and accounting ... She believed that I should start my own business and liked the idea of my being a business owner.

Another mother was a full-time librarian; her daughter became a scientist: "She typed my thesis but did not understand the work. She said that I had spent enough time in school and it was time to get a job."

At least two mothers secured critical interviews for their daughters. One woman told us: "My mother worked at a regional farmers market and talked about me with a professor from the university. She got me a job interview, and I was hired as an assistant professor." And for Mia, too, an interview arranged by her mother changed everything.

> I wanted to be a star.
>
> Mia, *customer service professional, hospitality industry*

The daughter of Italian immigrants, Mia was first in her family to go to college. Because she was a talented singer, she aspired to be a star and pursued a degree in music. However, her professional interests took a dramatic turn. After an interview for a part-time job, arranged by her mother, she was offered a position with a major hotel and found she loved it. She believed the experiences of growing up in an Italian family and serving as a high school teaching assistant were important influences in her career in the hospitality industry, where she enjoyed mentoring, teaching, and seeing herself and others develop. Mia worked for several exclusive hotels and private clubs. Overseeing service in five hotels, she was responsible for bringing corporate operating procedures into local service training. Later, she served on a task force charged with opening new hotels, including one in Palm Springs, California, where she found it very exciting to watch both the project and the team develop and evolve. Mia said she was always comfortable in her own skin. When she was asked as a young mother, "What do you do?" she would answer, "I'm a mother and I work at ..." Reflecting on her professional life today, she continued, "My career has not and does not define me as a person. I have always been a confident person aspiring to be the best that I could be on all levels. I have had many successes in both 'the supporting role' as well as the 'star.' " Mia and her husband relocated several times in their careers, and as they both approached the end of their last appointments, her biggest question was "Where do we go from here ... I need to find the rhythm for what's next." She did not see herself slowing down and did not want to be seen as "an old lady with no value." As she said, "It has become important to know my own worth." It was also very important to her to stay current, both in her field and with world events. She didn't like the word "retirement," but she was "not afraid to be idle for a day." And as much as Mia loved being a grandmother, she was certain she didn't want to be a childcare provider.

"Was your father influential in your career decision?" Although slightly over half of the women answered yes, the nature of their fathers' influence took many forms. Some fathers offered unqualified support and deliberately groomed their daughters for careers. Other fathers insisted their daughters have a financial safety net or backup plan to marriage.

Fathers who championed and supported their daughters came from a variety of professions:

> Bank executive: He always assumed I would have a career and was my source of advice when I had a business issue that I needed help with.
>
> Government auditor: He wanted me to be an anchor on TV news—he said that was my calling. At the same time, he thought working for the U.S. government would provide enormous security, for which he was grateful.
>
> Vice president of a toy company: Once, he said perhaps I should study something useful (accounting instead of Italian, which I'd proposed, but did not do), but he never interfered in my decisions, nor helped me make them, that I recall.
>
> Insurance manager: My father supported me in everything I did. He told me I could be the best, and he always wanted to know what I was doing even though he could not understand my work.

In the following profiles, we learn how three fathers offered their daughters different kinds of positive encouragement.

I followed my passion.

Emmy, *scientist in an international corporation*

The daughter of a librarian and an insurance manager, Emmy grew up near a Strategic Air Command base and was deeply affected by the sight of the Atlas rocket explosion in 1961. "What can I do?" she asked her father. He responded, "Do very well in school, especially math and science," and this response unwittingly became the basis of her career. As she described it, she never really decided on a career path but followed her passion. She earned degrees in chemistry and became a scientist, conducting research on the structure of molecules and eventually running labs worldwide for a major corporation. After an LGBT conference, she connected with another woman in her company who had also attended, and although at first they were not protected within the company or the state where they lived, she and others built a business plan for the company in support of LGBT equity in the workplace. The company was eventually recognized as one of the first to earn 100 percent on the Corporate Equality Index. As Emmy described it, that journey put her in contact with all of the corporate leadership. Emmy spoke fondly of the scientists she worked with, describing them as intuitive and compassionate. She said she missed the people and the nutty ideas. In retirement, she was doing consulting, helping family members who had a chronic illness, caring for her grandchildren, and working in their classrooms. Emmy liked being physically active. She loved to use tools and build and design things. Her passion and interest in the future excited her and moved her forward. For Emmy, spiritual awareness was paramount, both as a need and a driver of the work we do following retirement. As she explained, "Spiritual awareness for me has its groundings in compassion. Compassion for people's lot in life as well as how they express themselves through their thoughts and deeds, truly believing that we need to care for all people and we need to help all people find their deep inner meaning and connection to others."

He was a champion of women.

Reid, *marketing and executive recruiting professional*

Reid's mother was a teacher, and her father was a general in the U.S. Air Force whom she describes simply as "a champion of women and education." Reid was raised with the philosophy that "people are all equal," a belief she credits to her father's military career. She said it was a nonissue in her family that she would go to college and graduate school. "Everyone was expected to come to dinner with questions and to engage in lively conversation. Education was more important than money, and having a productive life was most important." Reid earned an undergraduate degree in nutrition but found that the only jobs available were in hospitals. Looking for more opportunities, she earned her MS and MBA degrees simultaneously. She was one of the few women in her MBA program, where she took classes with astronauts who were also earning MBAs. However, as she pointed out, they had secretaries to type their papers. Reid went on to become one of the first females with an MBA hired by her company. Even though discrimination was sometimes "in her face"—for instance, she was not allowed to answer the phone because her male colleagues' wives would wonder who was there—she had to "let it go." She said she never bought into the feeling that she was being discriminated against. "If you focus on yourself and do what you're supposed to do and excel, you will be rewarded." Reid's real professional love was marketing. She considered executive recruiting a form of marketing, and ten years earlier, she had cofounded a company devoted to consulting, coaching, and recruiting. She saw younger professionals trying to balance their family, children, and career and said the dynamics hadn't really changed. "If you want to have a family you actually *see,* you have to make decisions. You can't have it all, or you will have regrets."

My father took me under his wing.

Nour, *journalist and humanitarian for an international organization*

Nour was born into a Palestinian refuge family in Tripoli, where she lived until the mid-1950s. Her family members, fortunate to be naturalized Lebanese citizens, were eventually reunited in Beirut. As Nour matured into an independent and curious young person, her mother pressed her father, a physician, to take an active role in mentoring and guiding her. When Nour was eight, her father taught her English so she could answer the phone. As an older teenager, she assisted him in his medical practice during the summer. She first considered becoming a doctor but had second thoughts after accompanying her father to observe some surgeries. "My mother was a combination of opposites: seemingly a doll on a pedestal, very pretty with uniquely blue eyes, petite, and helpless. She also took over my father's finances at a critical time, and was always thought to be at the edge of innovative things." Nour's education in Beirut included time spent in French, Lebanese, and English systems. She attended the American University of Beirut, a "melting pot, with a very progressive reputation." After a two-year period of exploration, Nour took up journalism at the suggestion of her mother. During her interview, Nour vividly recalled her work as a United Press International (UPI) journalist during the Lebanese Civil War: "There were not many women, but there was no space for gender politics." At the end of her twelve-hour shift, she would drive to her family's home, where only the beloved cook and nanny of thirty years and the traumatized family dog remained. When Nour's mother visited, she would "go crazy with worry," thinking of Nour commuting alone at midnight under the shelling and through armed checkpoints. After five years, Nour knew she had to get out and left for the United States to earn a master's degree. In Beirut, she had begun working for a large international organization. After finishing her master's, she was recommended for another position in the organization, where her career focused on humanitarian and child rights issues as well as internal gender and diversity policies. After her retirement, she found time to reflect and connect to what she called "the essence of who I am, not the layers of what was added by years and a multiplicity of roles."

When it came to ensuring their daughters had a backup plan, fathers from across the professions encouraged their daughters to be practical. The advice of this woman's father, a lawyer, was echoed by many others:

> Early on, it was clear that I should find a career that was practical and where there were a lot of jobs. I don't know that I ever heard him say "Be a teacher," but there was not a strong support for exploring nontraditional careers for women at that point in time.

Some fathers served as explicit role models, as this woman's father did in his job as a mail carrier:

> He influenced me through his example of sticking with a steady job that allowed him enough energy to do agricultural chores and other pursuits. His job allowed him to retire at age fifty-five, with his years of service counting towards his thirty-five years. Perhaps this was more a lifestyle and financial planning influence than purely a career influence, but it was an admirable example to me.

One characteristic shared by all of the women in Cohort 25 was that they had siblings, yet there were many differences in family dynamics. As we see in the women's profiles, when there were sons, the education and careers of the boys were often a primary focus in the family, both in terms of attention and financial support. Siblings were mentioned in other contexts as well, including competitiveness.

When we asked, "Were you competitive as a child?" most women answered yes. Some described themselves as competing with their siblings; others said they were competitive by nature or competed primarily with themselves. Often, academics were mentioned, but sports and other extracurricular activities were important, too. Women described their competitiveness in different ways, but they remembered it well: "I had a very smart older brother and thought I needed to achieve as well academically. I played sports, but wasn't super competitive. I was an overachiever. Pushing myself"; "I wanted to always be better than my sister. She is six years older than I am and we were not close growing up but she always challenged me"; "I competed in a variety of 4-H events but not sports, since there were not any available until Title IX came along after I graduated"; and "I cared a good deal as a younger child about getting top grades, getting into top programs in high school, getting into a good college. Once in college, I became much less competitive. I became very social, and I did not have focused career goals that would have stimulated me to stand out academically."

In answer to the question, "Was your family active in the community?" a pattern emerged of families committed to church, school, and charitable activities. Almost three-quarters of the women said their families were active or somewhat active. Several women's responses illustrated the range and consistency of community involvement from family to family: "My mother was active in church and local hospitals. My father in Masons, Rotary and running charitable fundraising for the March of Dimes"; "[My family was] active in our synagogue, local sports, school activities, volunteering for social causes"; "Both were active as presidents in religious sisterhoods, men's groups, PTA (Parent Teacher Association), sports, and other community activities"; "My father provided free medical services to disadvantaged populations. My mother was involved in organizing charitable events"; and "We were a military family and moved every two to three years. There are expectations on military families to do charity/community work."

PURSUING A CAREER: WHAT WERE THE EXPECTATIONS?

Despite the fact that most of the mothers who worked held positions in traditional fields, when we asked, "Was your career direction based on expectations that as a woman you would go into a traditional field, such as teaching, social work, or nursing?" over half of the women

answered no. This woman described her parents' response to her decision to attend art school: "Neither parent discouraged my decision to
go to art school, but it was foreign to them and they didn't know
how I would be able to support myself. After I was successful in my
business they were very proud of me."

The percentage of women answering yes rose when we asked, "Was
it expected that you would go to college, then get married?" However,
a third of the women indicated that marriage was not seen as the *only*
expectation after high school.

> That I would go to college and have a career and possibly do graduate
> school was a given. Pressure to marry from the family was not overt,
> or perhaps I've forgotten. Societal pressure to marry was so strong that
> family pressure was not particularly necessary. My nonchalance regard-
> ing not being married, as well as the family's, was probably due to their
> not being concerned that I would attract someone—and they rarely
> liked my boyfriends.

When asked, "What were your reasons for pursuing a career?" over
half the women agreed that they were inspired by the feminist movement of the 1960s. How that inspiration was manifested was as individual as each woman. Some gained confidence from a new sense of
empowerment. Others identified with the call for action and change,
as demonstrated by comments such as these from a lawyer and a
human resources professional: "We had a loud voice and change was
afoot. It was okay to be outspoken" and "I wanted to impact others
as a competent woman."

For many women, changes brought by expanding rights and opportunities had a profound effect on their professional lives.

> Our opportunities allowed us to get spunky.
>
>   Susan, *physician and entrepreneur*

Susan said she never knew what she was going to be when she grew
up, but she always loved science. Her father had quit high school at
sixteen to join the navy during World War II, and in her family, education was seen as the key to the world. With that conviction, and the
supportiveness of her parents, Susan always thought she could do
whatever she wanted to do. She went to a private women's college,
became a biology major, and then aimed to get a PhD in physiology
to pursue research. When one of her mentors, a research professor,
told her to get an MD or an MD/PhD because it was easier to get grant
money, Susan applied to medical school. In med school she became

hooked on the clinical sciences, and after her second year, she no longer pursued research. She loved the challenge of being a female in the medical school, where fewer than 20 percent of the students in her class were women. She started out in primary care but shifted to radiology, where she enjoyed working with both patients and other doctors. Her entrepreneurial spirit led to her creating an innovative business partnership in 1983. Susan said, "Even though we were in the vanguard, the work was out there for us. Our opportunities allowed us to get spunky. But with that spunkiness, competence was essential. We had to be educated and willing to take risks." Recently retired at the time of her interview, Susan said she was very busy and spontaneous, enjoying life and taking a full year to "say no to everything." Each year she continued to get together with a group of nine women she had known and remained friends with since college.

For some women, the influence of feminism was the fundamental message of independence, as this woman put it: "I was inspired by the concept of independence ... Not being dependent on anyone. Also, the concept that women are qualified to do anything in the work place—not just become teachers and nurses."

Elaborating on the inspiration of the feminist movement, women mentioned specific cultural touchstones that added to the momentum of feminism in the 1970s. One was Marlo Thomas's 1972 album *Free to Be ... You and Me*, which was in Thomas's own words, "a children's record created to expel the gender and racial stereotypes of the era, while rewriting all those pat 'happily ever afters' that dominated the fairy tales of our youth."[1] While children were the primary audience for Thomas's popular recording, spin-off book, and television special, another source of inspiration, the Boston Women's Health Book Collective publication *Our Bodies, Ourselves* (1973), was directed specifically toward adult women. The book encouraged women to learn about their bodies. In the 1973 preface, the connection between knowledge of the body and personal freedom is made clear: "Learning to understand, accept, and be responsible for our physical selves, we are freed of some of these preoccupations and can start to use our untapped energies."[2] Women in our study referred to book groups— now long-standing—that began by meeting to talk about *Our Bodies, Ourselves* when it first came out.

EARNING A LIVING

The women of Cohort 25 all had an early, internalized sense of why they wanted to pursue a career. Although the direction they would go in might have been unclear at the beginning, they almost all spoke of being driven, inspired, of *wanting something that was meaningful for them*. The thing they were striving for took different forms, but the force it exerted over their education and career paths was irrefutable. They knew more opportunities were available to them than had been available to their mothers and grandmothers, and although they might not have articulated it, they knew the world was opening up to them in new ways. The pleasure of the work itself and the drive to move ahead began to characterize the careers of these Baby Boomer women early in their lives.

"Needed to earn a living" was chosen by three-quarters of the women as a reason for pursuing a career. As one woman remembered, "My husband and I were going to get married, and he was in professional school and I needed to earn a living to pay our expenses." For some women, the compulsion of *needing* to work involved much more than earning a salary. Another said, "I needed to work for my own satisfaction."

A third woman described the drive that motivated her, despite the financial support she was receiving for her graduate studies:

> I was driven, rather than needed, to earn a living, although in graduate school I was initially fully supported by a National Endowment for the Humanities fellowship and then a teaching fellowship.

She explained further:

> Money was not a driver, largely because I hadn't done the analysis needed. I wasn't oriented to do that; even though my family might have wished I'd done so, they never sat me down to do it. Lord knows, my university did nothing to ensure that its female students understood the ways of the world; or if they did, I was unaware of it.

Pursuing a career carried with it the expectations of others and a compelling sense of responsibility, as these women made clear: "In addition to being a wife and mother, I was always expected to realize my full potential using my God-given talents" and "My parents deserved to see my success."

Sometimes the strong, positive motivation for pursuing a career originated in a person's realizing what she did *not* want to do. Two women made the point emphatically: "I did not want to be a housewife" and "I knew I sure as hell wasn't going to be a farmer."

CAREER COUNSELING

When asked, "Did you have any career or guidance counseling at the high school level or during college?" women indicated that, if anything, the counseling they received tempered their ambitions. Only one woman said she had received career counseling in high school. Eight women had no counseling, and the rest said they received "minimal career counseling." Some were specifically discouraged from pursuing male-dominated professions such as medicine or were directed toward paths considered less challenging: "I attended an all-girls academic high school. I was not 'Ivy League' material and was counseled to go to a 'lesser' school and get financial aid."

In an era before the elaborate process of college searches and campus visits existed, students often applied to a college without having much information. Not knowing how or where to find programs that interested them led to unexpected detours. One woman recalled applying to college without realizing what the degree it advertised actually entailed:

> I always wanted to be a writer so I chose a college that listed a journalism major. As it turned out, the focus was on printing and the school dropped journalism within the year. Though printing courses were challenging, I was so excited about being away from home ... I spent the balance of the year taking courses and searching for what I wanted to do.

Another found her future career path by following a friend:

> There were no artists in my family, just working class and engineers. Then a friend who was very talented took me along when she went to look at art schools. Things happened and evolved. It was serendipitous.

After Baby Boomer women enrolled in college, the career counseling they received continued to be skimpy. Despite the fact that they would go on to have successful careers and earn a variety of advanced degrees, the women of Cohort 25 received very little help from college advisors or counselors. Only one woman said she received career counseling during college; fourteen received none, and the rest said the career counseling they received was minimal. Women also described missing out on opportunities for networking while in college or graduate school. Although the word was not yet in use, the principles of networking were certainly being modeled for men, as this anecdote illustrated:

> I did not seek it; was it available? I recall a male classmate, now a TV producer, showing me a letter he was writing to an ad firm, saying that

"Mr. So-and-So" recommended he write to them. Somehow, I did not learn the lesson of that. My department head got me an internship and recommended me for a summer program and graduate school. He'd noticed me in a small graduate course he gave and which I aced. I recall his advice being more reactive than pro-active.

"Was there a particular person who influenced your professional interests and direction?" Three-quarters of the women answered yes, and of those, the majority identified family members, teachers, or professors. For these women, the influence of their family members was both inspirational and practical: "My father always talked about coming to this country without knowing what the future would hold. He always said, 'You've got the world by a string ... take it'" and "An aunt and uncle encouraged me to attend a business college and then mentored me as I entered the workforce."

Go as far as you can, but don't dabble.
                    Angel, *teacher, musician, coach, and human resources professional*

Angel grew up on the campus of an all-black land grant college in Alabama, where both of her parents were educators and musicians. Her family and the environment in which she grew up exerted a powerful influence over who she became, what she did, and the choices she made. She said she got her juggling skills from her father, observing how he handled his many roles as pastor, chaplain, music director, and professor. Her mother, too, served as a model for balancing family and professional responsibilities: "My mother was the head of music education, taught, raised a family, and directed the university choir." Trained as a classical musician from a young age, Angel was expected to go to college and continue her study of music. She described herself as always being interested in many things. Her parents never discouraged her interests, but she was, instead, encouraged to go as far as she could and "not dabble." After college, Angel took a teaching position in which she traveled from school to school and taught music to 1,400 children each week. Although she was glad to have had the experience, she decided to go back to school, where she planned to continue her musical training at the graduate level. In graduate school, she realized she had a strong interest in and affinity for counseling, so she added that direction to her professional focus. Her combination of strengths in music, education, and counseling prepared her well for positions that ranged from college recruiting and career consulting, to director of human resources at a major foundation. When asked about her move from academia into the corporate arena, she said, "I learned an amazing amount about me, the world, the corporate world, and companies and how they are run ... it was one of the most monumental points of my career." At the time of her interview, she was enjoying her current position, where her range of experience had made her an ideal candidate: "I was strong *and* soft. I could counsel people and also make decisions and problem solve." In addition to working full-time, Angel continued to perform and had recently sung in a special concert in Carnegie Hall. As she anticipated retirement, she was looking forward to traveling and spending time with her family. Her elderly parents would have loved for her to move back to Alabama, a move she said she might consider.

OTHER INFLUENCES

Beyond their families and in the absence of formal career counseling, where did the influences come from that encouraged and inspired these early Baby Boomer women? One woman said, "I did not have a single mentor, but was driven more by something internal. I was once told I was ambitious." Often, a woman encountered, studied, or worked with someone early in her career who exerted a significant influence over her decisions and direction and became a role model.

> My first model of a woman balancing career and family
>
> Margaret, *university administrator*

Margaret grew up in a family where working hard, doing well, and taking an active part in the community were all important values. Her father was a lawyer; her mother had graduated from a private women's college and was a champion golfer. From a young age, Margaret was a competitive athlete; she credited the sports emphasis on teamwork, withstanding pressure, and leadership with being very formative in her development. Early in her career she met a female physician with six children who wore two pagers, one for her family and one for her patients. Margaret realized then that women were looking for ways to have both personal and professional lives. Rising through several administrative positions at a large university, Margaret spent most of her forty-year career in higher education administration, where she said she enjoyed leading people by letting them be creative. When she retired, she felt good about the body of work she had accomplished, especially the creation of groundbreaking judicial education programs. But she was also burned out, tired of the lack of support from men in leadership roles. Having spent many years at the university, she knew it was time to leave. "Time is precious and limited, and I want to make the most of what lies ahead," she noted. After she retired, she became actively involved in helping her children and grandchildren. She also oversaw the building of a second home, served on the board of directors of a community music organization, and took on other volunteer projects. At the time of her interview, she was eager to step back from some of her many volunteer activities and devote more time to a single project aimed at keeping college alumni in the community after they graduate. She hoped to do this by connecting young people to resources and opportunities while they were still in college.

Another woman recognized that although she did not ask for career help, she later found a valuable resource in a personal relationship:

> I was mostly self-directed during the first part of my career ... Although I talked a lot with close friends, I don't recall that these discussions helped me to problem solve with regard to my career, but these must have been of some help ... I never asked for direction; I asked for and received advocacy but not mentoring. When I got engaged my fiancé and then-husband became a major influence.

Occasionally, the influence on a woman's professional interests and direction was serendipitous and might have gone unnoticed by the person who was actually making a difference in the life of the young woman. Two of the lawyers in Cohort 25 described how they made the decision to go to law school while working at other jobs—waitressing and doing routine office work—where each observed firsthand the power and respect given to lawyers.

> The lawyers I knew were shocked!
>
> Vera, *lawyer, technology specialist, and writer*

Vera did not remember having a calling when she was young, but she said she could not imagine not working and supporting herself. Her mother was a teletypesetter for a newspaper, and her father worked for the U.S. Postal Service. Reflecting, Vera said her high school English teacher probably encouraged her interest in writing. Vera's first job after college was as an eighth-grade language arts teacher. After relocating to be with her husband, she tried substitute teaching but realized that at twenty dollars a day, she could make more money waiting on tables, so she went to work as a waitress and bartender in a local restaurant, where many lawyers—all male—came for lunch. Vera was "champing at the bit for more education" and

Table 2.1   Family Backgrounds and Choosing Careers

Mothers' backgrounds	Some were college educated with careers in teaching and nursing; some worked full-time for government or were active partners in family business; others were homemakers involved in community or religious organizations
Fathers' backgrounds	Some worked for corporations; others were employed in education, law, government, health care, and military; many were self-employed, owning businesses or family farms
Siblings	100%
Competitiveness	64% included siblings, self, academics, sports, and extracurricular activities
Factors that shaped family culture and values	Family-owned business, military career, tradition of teaching and service, refugees or Holocaust survivors, strong religious or ethnic identities
Mothers who worked/had a career	40% full-time 20% part-time
Mothers' full-time jobs	Teachers, farmers, college professor, teletypesetter, switchboard operator, librarian, department supervisor for federal government
Mothers' influence in their careers	60%
Fathers' influence in their careers	56%
Families active in their communities	40% yes 32% somewhat
Implicitly understood that they would go to college	84%
Expected to go to college and then get married	64% said yes but wasn't the only expectation; career and graduate school were other considerations

(*continued*)

Table 2.1 Family Backgrounds and Choosing Careers (*continued*)

Expected to become a teacher, social worker, or nurse	56% no 44% yes
Reason for pursuing a career	76% to earn a living 60% inspired by the feminist movement of the 1960s
Career or guidance counseling in high school or college	60% said minimally in high school and 56% said none in college
Influenced in professional interests and direction	75% said yes and identified family members, teachers, and professors
Early idea of what would be exciting career	60%

realized she could use the research and writing skills she enjoyed in a career in law. To the astonishment of the lawyers who were her customers, she applied and was accepted to law school. One of the attorneys even insisted her acceptance letter had to be a fake. After graduating, Vera went to work for a legal publishing company, where her interests in keeping up with technology and helping others were critical factors in her advancement. As she described it, once the publishing company moved into an electronic medium, "the playing field was leveled for women because the technology was new for everyone." In twenty years with the company, she held several different positions. "That suited me well, as I would be ready for something new every three years or so. I became known for working with employees to change their skill sets while eliminating outdated tasks and departments." After her career in legal publishing, she worked for an independent literary publishing company, receiving what she calls "a degree in nonprofit." A part-time freelance writer after she retired, Vera focused on human interest stories that made a connection to the legal community. She was recognized by her peers as a mentor for young women lawyers, but she was quick to tell young women, "Be sure you like what you're doing. Explore other things that could be options. Be sure money isn't the only thing that drives you."

Family influences certainly were important in the education, and sometimes in the career paths, of the women in Cohort 25. Other adults outside their immediate families occasionally exerted an influence on their education and career decisions, sometimes even unwittingly. The most important point about the influences on the women of Cohort 25 is that from a young age, these women learned to carve out their own path. They had a strong personal sense of identity, and they knew they were going to do meaningful things with their lives. Sometimes, their dreams were supported by their families; sometimes, as young women, they simply had to make their own way. They tuned out negative or unhelpful comments, and, when possible, gravitated instead toward individuals whose support they knew intuitively they could count on.

NOTES

1. Marlo Thomas, "Free to Be . . . You and Me—Forty Years Later," *The Blog* (blog), *Huffington Post*, November 30, 2012, updated January 30, 2013, http://www.huffingtonpost.com/marlo-thomas/free-to-be-40-years-later_b_2206066.html.

2. Boston Women's Health Book Collective, *Our Bodies, Ourselves: A Book by and for Women* (New York: Simon & Schuster, 1973), 3.

3

Building Careers in
an Era of Change

How did the women of Cohort 25 begin to know what they wanted to do professionally? They were curious, high achieving, and looking for ways to earn a living that would take them beyond the fields that had been available to women. (See Table 3.1: Careers.) We asked the women to think back and reflect on their early ideas about a career. "Did you have an early subliminal idea of what would be exciting for you in a career?" Over half said yes. Ranging from intuitive to pragmatic, the women's responses demonstrated a level of self-awareness that continued to affect how they talked about their careers. Two women described their early career ideas very differently: "Freedom and variety were essential components of any job. Also, recognition was an important piece of the puzzle" and "In retrospect, my mother's interest in the stock market and the overall discussion of business issues in the home influenced my interest in business and finance." A third woman spoke of an early epiphany: "When I first visited the organization . . . everything was beautiful. There was diversity, of people—and clothing—from all over the world, as well as lots of political hope. I knew then and said to myself: *This is where I want to be.*"

> Then I began to *aspire* to things.
>
> Sara, *museum curator*

Sara grew up in Newton, Massachusetts, which she later recognized as an "education-privileging place." Her mother was a teacher and her father a lawyer, but as Sara said, rather than encouraging an interest in curiosity or experimentation, "the message of my childhood, in the 1940s and '50s, was 'do well in school and be a good girl.'" She loved to read and became an English major, but the "other track of the story," as she described it, was her subliminal exposure to cultural richness, especially through the books on artists and paintings given to her by her mother. As a young woman, she did not see that there might be a connection between liking art and identifying something she might do professionally. Sara said it took her a long time to experience the spark of meaningful work and that she feels she was intellectually and academically immature at first. She attended a small private women's college, where she occasionally wrote a campus column for the local newspaper. After college, she taught for a few years and then, during her husband's medical training, learned about and completed a graduate program in museum studies. For the first time, she imagined a career in which her interests and enthusiasm could be aligned. She remembered how she "began to *aspire* to things." When they relocated for her husband's residency, she volunteered in a school arts enrichment program offered by an art museum in western New York State. Over the years, Sara moved from being a volunteer to serving as a part-time curator of education and eventually chief curator, a job she enjoyed and to which she dedicated herself wholeheartedly. She left her position after she began to consider how many more years she might have for herself and her family and weighed that against the time invested in aspects of her job that were unsatisfying. She talked easily about the psychological adjustment of "no longer having your own sandbox" and tended not to think about being retired. Sara was continuing to work on a research project she had started before her retirement, curating a large and previously unstudied group of archival materials held in several different collections, with the goal of uniting them online for public access. When people asked what she was doing, she replied, "I have a *really* big project I am very excited about."

BEING THE FIRST OR THE ONLY

As we saw in Chapter 1, many women were the first or the only female in a company, or position, or team. In their interviews, they often spoke about these "firsts" with pride, especially their achievements as girls.

My own tools, my own business.

Kelly, *artist and business owner*

Kelly grew up playing with boys and having a lot of freedom. She never thought about differences between boys and girls, and her parents never made her feel a girl had to be a certain way. She always liked to save money, and as the first girl in town with a paper route, she delivered newspapers to sixty customers in two blocks. Her father was an engineer who did and fixed everything, with Kelly working right alongside him. "When I came home from college and asked for a toolbox, he probably wondered what he had done!" Kelly also loved sailing and working on wooden boats. Her first job was in a boatyard, where the owner reached out to her, knowing she was in art school and familiar with boats. After that, she became the first female in several boatyards, working as a boat carpenter. She always knew she didn't want to work in an office or have a nine-to-five lifestyle, but in art school, she had heard the message, "Women can't have a creative life because all their creativity goes into having children." When she needed an income after completing graduate school, she set about creating her own clothing line. Kelly discovered she liked the business part as much as the creative part of her work. She also realized that all of her former jobs had helped prepare her for having her own business, including time spent working in the college admissions office, where she learned about "selling," and waitressing, where she honed her people skills. At the time of her interview, the hardest thing for Kelly was not having a way to refer to herself. As she described it, "retired" and "semi-retired" wouldn't work, so she had "grabbed on to the word 'transitioning,'" which worked well since she couldn't be specific about what was next for her. Kelly added, "You have to come to the point where you recognize you are valid without working." She was very interested in doing her own artwork now, for pure creation rather than as a business. She had been encouraged to write, but the sitting involved was not as appealing as the physical experience of making art. For Kelly's sixtieth birthday, her friends gave her a gift card to a hardware store to buy the table saw she wanted.

JUMPING IN

With a combination of education and self-confidence, women were emboldened to jump in and take positions in which they could learn and be successful. Many described taking a job that was a stretch or stepping into a brand-new environment, where confidence and persistence carried them forward. One spoke of the "optimistic premise" that always led her to believe "I think I can do it."

I saw their humanity, and knew I could connect.

Lola, *psychoanalyst*

Lola said all of the characters in her family history played a part in influencing her career path. Her parents both fled Poland, where her father had been a teacher, and met in Siberia when they were imprisoned in labor camps during World War II. After the war, they were married in a camp in Paris and received a one-year scholars visa to come to the United States. They immediately conceived Lola so that she would be born in the States and the family would be allowed to stay. As other Jewish Germans and Poles were doing, Lola's parents bought a chicken farm in New Jersey, despite the fact that they spoke no English and knew nothing about chickens. They liked having no one to answer to and overcame significant losses, including a catastrophic flood, to become very successful. Lola said her parents raised her not to trust others, especially people who said they were their friends. She learned early to be the person others approached to talk about their problems. She summed it up this way: "Focus on the other, be sure everyone is okay, don't cause any trouble." Her intuitive ability to connect to others became the basis of her profession, starting with her first work-study placement at age nineteen, when, with absolutely no background, she was assigned to work with a group of severely mentally ill patients. At first unsuccessful in her attempts to find a job in social services, after college she took a secretarial job at a major teaching hospital. In six months, Lola was offered the position of intake coordinator of the outpatient psychiatry clinic, where she interviewed new patients and matched them with psychology interns and psychiatry residents for treatment. Then she was promoted to a position in which she helped therapists develop plans for working with patients, in what she calls her "best job ever." Eventually, Lola was allowed to work under supervision with patients and was encouraged to go to graduate school. She earned an MSW and went on to become certified in psychoanalysis. Lola moved into private practice when she was pregnant in the mid-1980s. After that, she continued in private practice but had to start over a couple of times because of family moves. For Lola, the most exciting part of her work in mental health was making a difference in people's lives. After moving twice across the country, she and her husband settled in New Jersey, where she was teaching and her practice was growing. Lola described having a nice balance between work and leisure, adding, "I have *zero* to complain about."

Another woman gave an example of the determination and confidence she brought to her career. After working at the National Endowment for the Humanities, she moved to a new city, where she found it difficult to get an interview. She decided to sit and wait in an office at a public television station until someone would agree to meet with her.

Her persistence paid off: "They needed someone to do fundraising, and although I never had raised a cent, in fact, in my previous position, I had given money away, I knew I could learn to do it."

Women in Cohort 25 not only jumped in and figured out how to be successful, but they also brought new ideas and entrepreneurial energy to the workplace. Several described striking out on their own, starting businesses, and establishing professional practices. Although support and encouragement came from many directions, the women also faced resistance.

Sometimes, it was tough to sell a new idea, no matter how successful it later turned out to be.

> I wasn't afraid.
>
> Pauline, *sales professional and entrepreneur*

Pauline left her hometown at age seventeen and lived on a kibbutz in Israel for five years. On her return to the United States, she took a job in sales for a major corporation. Pauline credited her years in Israel with developing her confidence. "I had seen so much horrific stuff, I wasn't afraid." She came up with an idea for bringing services directly to customers and, unable to garner interest or support from her supervisor, started her own business in 1985. She applied for and received Women's Business Enterprise (WBE) Certification through a process that she describes as not difficult but very detailed and bureaucratic. As she said, "It was almost as though the auditor did not believe that one's business was legitimate." With an emphasis on developing her own staff, beginning with women in Harlem, Pauline became very successful in her business. She loved creating jobs for women and shattering stereotypes while also solving challenging business problems. Pauline valued innovation and independence and was not afraid of "C-Suite" or top senior-level executives. She was also very savvy. "When I had my business, I always dressed in a suit and put up my long hair. I knew how to blend, and had to keep my strong feminist inclinations to myself . . . I always found out if a man's wife stayed at home or had a career. This helped me understand men's attitudes and interaction with me." Pauline sold her business and relocated with her husband when he took a new position out of state. She found it shocking to suddenly discover that—as a corporate wife—she had become invisible. After returning to the area where she grew up, Pauline and her husband were facing the new challenge of his sudden disability. Although Pauline was very much involved in his care, she was on the lookout for new opportunities. As Pauline stressed, "The commodities I now have are time and energy." She wanted to use them carefully but said she could probably get energized to do something "big and loud."

DEVELOPING CAREERS

For young women establishing themselves in careers, changes going on outside the walls of universities, corporations, museums, studios, and government offices had a powerful effect. What did the careers of Cohort 25 women look like as they grew and took shape? What kept them going? What excited them? When and how did they make career moves? We asked women to look back on their careers, to think about the interruptions, the opportunities, and the point at which they realized they had found a fulfilling professional match.

"Did you have a period(s) of career interruption?" Two-thirds answered yes in response to this question. Eight women had taken maternity leave, and five referred to periods of unemployment. Apart from career interruptions to have or raise children, the periods when women were not working were often spent in preparing for a career change, relocating, or going back to school. "I had two brief periods of career interruption (less than four months) when a business closed and I was out of work" and "Unemployment—occasionally, several months, here and there. The major gap was for my MBA."

Another woman described how her husband's career moves interrupted as well as influenced her career: "When we moved to follow my husband's career, typically I needed to find a new source of employment. Also, at a certain point I knew that I did not want to pursue a teaching career, and as we were also moving, I stopped working as I figured out next steps."

"Did you have periods of restlessness during specific jobs?" Again, two-thirds answered yes. Two women had different thoughts on restlessness: "I always wanted to be self-employed or have control over my schedule" and "Aspects of my museum/exhibits jobs were not enjoyable. I was dissatisfied, but not restless. Restless would have been more healthy."

Motivated by novelty.

Barb, *professor and university administrator*

Barb was raised on a farm located in a village on the Erie Canal. As a girl, she was advised by her mother to get a career, "because you can't count on a man to support you." She was always interested in education, and in college, she says, "I discovered I had an intellect." Barb became interested in psychology and undertook a significant research project while still an undergraduate. After earning a PhD, she was hired by a large private university for a teaching position in the College of Business. At the time, the male faculty members outnumbered the female professors ten to one. Barb spent her career in higher education, both as a professor and an administrator, and said she was happiest when she was working with a woman mentor and exposed to the broader academic community and more female colleagues through a campus-wide strategic planning process. Opportunities came her way as a result of that project, allowing her to exercise and expand her skills in organization and administration. At the recommendation of her mentor, Barb attended the Bryn Mawr HERS (Higher Education Resource Services) program in leadership development. She then went on to serve as associate dean in her home college, and after developing a collaborative project with a colleague in another field, she switched colleges within the same university to take on a new codirector appointment. Barb admitted to getting bored easily and having her own "five-year rule" of needing to move on to new challenges. What interested her most was "having agency and the recognition of achievement." In order to gain that kind of recognition, she believed it was necessary to make new moves. Asked what most motivated her, she replied, "Novelty." Barb was concerned about how to replicate the "greenhouse environments" and affiliations of the university after she retired. "I'm trying to stay patient," she said. "I'm not finished yet."

CAREER OPPORTUNITIES

In response to the question, "Did your job or role change as a result of opportunities?" the majority of the women answered yes. When we asked, "Do you feel your opportunities were the result of luck?" over half of the women said yes or somewhat. Although some women credited luck with bringing them opportunities, other factors received much more attention. For example, as one woman described it, "I'd say serendipity—timing, enough persistence and coinciding trends— more than luck, but luck is important."

The numbers rose when we asked, "Do you feel your career opportunities were based on your networking?" Here, all but two of the women answered yes or somewhat. But luck and networking were only two sources of opportunity. When asked, women added many other examples of boosts to their careers that were personal to them.

It wasn't luck.

Mary, *science teacher, curriculum designer, and administrator*

As a girl, Mary loved school, especially science. Neither of her parents had had the opportunity to go to college, and Mary knew that her father, especially, would have loved it. He was very creative and worked his way up from being a cashier to being a branch manager in a major baked goods company. Although she was not employed outside their home, Mary's mother was "always out and doing things" as president of the garden club and golf league. Mary laughed as she recalled her experience of being a "first" in her community. "Between college and grad school, I had a job as a post office driver in my home-town. It shocked others to see me in the role—first female ever in that job." She began her career teaching advanced placement biology and then took ten years off to have three children. During that time, she created a science lab with materials that were going unused in her children's school. The success of her volunteer effort was enormous, and she was offered a position to develop the science curriculum for state education requirements. This was the first in a series of expand-ing career opportunities. The explosion of the Internet and growth of technology in education led to Mary's appointment as assistant super-intendent for technology in the district where she worked. In that role, she partnered with a regional museum and science center to develop, build, and write the curricula for complex science simulation projects. Mary described her career path, "My whole life was a series of doors opening." She didn't credit luck but said, "I applied myself, worked hard, volunteered for additional work, and went over and above job expectations." After taking an early retirement to help her elderly mother, Mary remained very active. She swam a mile every day and also loved golf and yoga. When talking about the commitment she made to care for her mother, Mary said, "I want to be able to look back and know I did all I could." She missed the creative part of her work and described the process she was going though as a "realignment," as she explored ways to find the focus and sense of accomplishment she had enjoyed in her career.

The list of other factors women cited as contributing to their career opportunities was extensive. Many personal strengths were seen as important, including knowing other languages, education, personal-ity, and "being willing to ask questions and learn."

Women also acknowledged the importance of how they were seen by others. For three women who made major career moves, their repu-tation and visibility were keys to moving ahead. The first woman moved from education, to human resources, to consulting sales as her career evolved: "I believe I had a good reputation in the workplace and was very much sought after by headhunters, especially in my forties." The second took her background in law into the corporate world, where, as she put it, "colleagues and acquaintances gave me encouraging feedback and allowed me to take on new responsibilities all the time; I was given roles that stretched me and gave me visibility/recognition." And the third woman, whose career spanned continents and disciplines, recognized the many ways in which reputation, as well as connections, advanced her career: "The people hiring me needed to think I had relevant ability and experience. There had to be enough in my resume and in the way I presented myself to get hired. Sometimes, the people hiring knew my track record, or had worked with me. Recommendations helped, often more than I realized at the time. I think people advocated for me. At least once, I was hired, in part, because the main decision maker had done graduate school where I did my BA."

Institutional changes created by training programs and new leadership also opened up opportunities, as one woman explained, "My first corporate career was with a large insurance company. In the '70s, they implemented a professional development initiative for women, and I was asked to participate in the program."

Other women described how opportunities came as a result of personal circumstances, whether through good fortune or out of necessity. For a curator, serendipity certainly played a part: "Being in the right place at the right time, which one could call luck, I suppose. I also was fortunate to have a boss who appreciated my strengths and was willing to overlook my somewhat nontraditional career path in my field." In another instance, change in an artist's personal life became the impetus for change in her career path: "Starting my business was out of necessity. I was in a marriage that was unhappy and needed to make money one way or the other."

A willingness to be open to new things, to be ready to seize opportunities as they arose, was seen as critical. A science educator described the opportunities she encountered with these words: "They were a challenge and a chance to improve myself."

I'll figure it out.

E.R., *university administrator and writer*

In answer to the question, "What inspired you?" E.R.'s answer was simple: "My mother." As E.R. described her, her mother was an educated, southern African American woman who raised three children alone. E.R.'s mother worked full-time as a department supervisor for the federal government, and as E.R. said, "My mother was my role model, but she definitely did not consider herself a feminist. I was gay and emerging from the closet, so I got very caught up in following news about the feminist movement and the gay liberation movement." While working at a student job in college, E.R. unexpectedly fell into a career she loved and a path that led to two master's degrees and positions of increasing responsibility in higher education academic affairs administration. "I really took to supervision roles and project management, wound up moving up the ranks, had lots of opportunities tossed my way to develop ideas, work with lots of different people, travel, do public speaking and deal with administrative tasks. I loved the people, the work, and the academic environment." E.R.'s career was driven by institutional commitment to innovation and technology and by her own entrepreneurial spirit. She was given several high-profile projects to manage, each requiring leadership and coordination spanning several sectors of the university and the community. As E.R. put it, her response to new opportunities had always been "Yes and I'll figure it out." A poet and spoken word artist, she often set aside some of her creative interests because of work and family demands but still continued writing and performing whenever possible. Still working at the time of her interview, she said it was very exciting and calming to anticipate being able to do more of her creative work when she retires—and to see where the creativity goes.

FINDING A DIRECTION

When women talked about their experiences as young girls, many said they felt the world was wide open to them and that they had boundless opportunities. How, and when, did they narrow the vast range of existing and emerging careers to find the right fit for their strengths and passions? How did the phrase "You can do anything you set your mind to" affect their decisions?

"At what point(s) in your career did you find a direction that would become fulfilling to you and match your interests and enthusiasms?" Some women said they quickly realized what direction they would be following: "Early on—after maternity leave"; "After college"; "From my first job in the mental health field on"; and "I was already having a great experience at work by the time I finished my first master's degree (two years after I finished my undergraduate work). The job suited me perfectly."

One woman even traced the origins of her career direction to events that occurred before her birth.

Before I was born ...

>   Bella, *psychologist, human resources professional, and executive coach*

Bella had been very focused from a young age. She always knew she wanted to work with people and always liked school. Because her parents were Holocaust survivors, she felt the defining moment in her life came before she was even born, when her parents came to the United States—"truly the land of milk and honey." They emphasized two things in their advice to her: "Never trust anyone" and "You can do whatever you want if you get an education." When asked if she had received any career guidance in high school, Bella answered, "Terrible experience. Said I should be a nurse or teacher even though I wanted to be an MD." She was told emphatically, "Girls become nurses, not doctors." Pursuing her interest in health care, Bella earned an MS in organizational development and organizational psychology. Beyond the academic credential, she referred to two other important results from her master's program: first, she learned work could be fulfilling, fun, and have an impact, and second, she came together with six other women to form a women's group that met weekly for twenty years. This group of women, who have discussed all aspects of life, continued to meet, although more sporadically, for forty years. Bella went on to earn a PhD in organizational psychology and to have a career that spanned many professional areas. She taught both high school and MBA students, worked for a medical equipment company, and ran her own executive coaching company. What she found most satisfying was having an impact on others, particularly when she could help people make a contribution to the greater good of their organizations while bettering themselves. Bella talked about the importance of having a balanced life and said her own experience was very important in her work with women clients. She was especially happy that her daughters were proud of her for what she had accomplished and that they had chosen exceptional careers and exceptional partners.

For Andy, finding her career direction meant taking a risk:

>   The biggest risk of my career—law school.
>
>   Andy, *lawyer and corporate business leader*

Andy grew up in a middle-class community outside Philadelphia, where her parents believed "the sky was the limit" for both Andy and her brother. Her parents kept a close eye on her, but she had freedom to explore as a girl. She was physically strong, athletic, and never liked to be confined. From the age of nine or ten, she was curious and looking for adventure. She saw school as a prison and couldn't wait to get out. Her mother worked in the corporate world and had no trust in it. She advised Andy: "The only way to make money and trust your job is to have your own business." Her father worked in government and was well aware of the many levels of bureaucracy. Andy said she pursued a career because she "had enormous self-confidence and loved taking risks." She considered going to law school the biggest risk she took in her career since she knew nothing about it, took the LSAT without studying, and was accepted. Her parents were thrilled by her decision to study law, knowing it was a "good credential" and would bring financial independence and respect. After law school, Andy created and ran the research department for a legal publishing company. When she later joined an executive outplacement firm as a business developer, she knew it would be a good fit: she was going to pursue legal clients; she had autonomy; she was getting terrific support; and she believed what she was selling was valuable. At the time of her interview, Andy had her own career counseling company, where she continued to network and meet interesting people. She loved "learning new stuff every single day" through the research she did for clients. Best of all, Andy said, "I can do it my way: no shackles!" When talking about the future, she was emphatic: "I'm not thinking about doing nothing. There's a lot that needs to be done to make things better." Andy said she would like to travel more and work with vulnerable animals, perhaps by running a shelter or sanctuary.

For others, finding a fulfilling direction involved embracing an evolving array of interests and having the energy to follow them.

> People realized I had gumption.
>
> Nancy, *entrepreneur, arts consultant, and author*

Nancy's mother was a homemaker and very encouraging of her daughter. From her, Nancy learned very early how to think strategically. She described herself as "self-competitive," even as a child. Nancy said that although being active in sports and having strong role models in their fathers may have been true of many women in this cohort, it was not the case for her. Her father provided another kind of inspiration, introducing her to a variety of community and cultural activities that included horseback riding, ice skating, and social dancing. Nancy said she was raised to be a wife and mother. She "fell into" her career quite unexpectedly, when her longtime boyfriend decided to marry someone else. In high school, she had taken some art classes at Carnegie Mellon University, but she knew she didn't have the patience for making art. After college, she was invited to be one of the first students in a new graduate-level museum studies program. This led to a high-profile job with a tremendous amount of responsibility in which she worked for a male mentor, although, as she pointed out, the word "mentor" wasn't being used at the time. Nancy said, "I found new directions along the entire sweep of my career. I have had a number of positions in government and nonprofits, and only once was I hired for a pre-existing job. In all other cases, the organization made up a new job for me. People would meet me and realize I had 'gumption.' They would put me in a job to do something they wanted to do but didn't have the staff for." Her gumption eventually led her to strike out on her own, even though when she told her boss she was leaving to start her own business, he responded, "You can't do that. Your husband won't like it." As she looked ahead, Nancy saw herself continuing to devote time to the same things that had interested her over the years but shifting how much time she devoted to each: writing, teaching, civic affairs, clients, and family. Nancy's husband was semiretired, so there was a "pull to do less," but, as she said, "When so many of my peers are winding down, I continue to feel like I'm winding up. Nobody gets to be our age who doesn't feel lucky to be able to continue to find clients and deliver quality work."

We still have a ton of energy.

Jenny, *hospital administrator and corporate operations professional*

Because of her dual interests during high school, Jenny was allowed to develop her own academic track of math/literature, whereas other students had to select either math/science or literature/writing. She excelled in math and wanted to be a high school math teacher, but college was out of the question since she had four brothers whose education took precedence. Instead, her family advised her to go to a two-year business school. Jenny started her career in a secretarial pool at Bell Labs and rose through the ranks. She moved on to become executive assistant to the president/CEO of a hospital and the administrative manager for the medical staff—an environment she loved and where she found her career direction in operations. As she described it, "My healthcare operations experience provided me with a broad scope of skills that easily made it adaptable to larger corporate environments." She was given a great deal of responsibility and aspired to the role of chief operations officer. However, working twelve-hour days, raising three children, and taking care of an elderly parent did not allow enough time for her to go back to college for the degree she would have needed. When the hospital where she was employed was closing, Jenny had the opportunity to work with an outplacement consultant. She soon realized that the outplacement industry would be a good match for her professionally, and she was hired to work for a competitor of the company she was first introduced to as a client. Having gone through multiple organizational changes during her years in the industry, she realized toward the end of her career that her professional experience was being seen as a drawback and that the new culture dismissed anyone who had been with the company ten years or more as being "old school" and not valued. Yet her view of the future remained optimistic: "Baby Boomers still have a ton of energy and intellectual resources. As technology advances, age isn't going to matter at all since people won't be visible." Jenny predicted this could be a reality in the next five years. Another change that she said she would like to see in the workplace was a new, accepted stage of employment for older workers in which their knowledge and experience were considered valuable assets to a company's success and bottom-line profits.

Finding a career direction occasionally came as a "Eureka!" moment when a specific position or a specific company provided the perfect fit, and with it came the realization *this is it*! One woman described it this way: "In 1983, I joined an outplacement firm as a consultant. It was a dream job." Another referred to a slower process but one that led just as surely to the realization she had found the ideal organization for her interests and expertise: "I worked steadily for two years as a consultant for the organization before they took me on full-time. That was the best match because of the cutting edge issues, colleagues and delegates, frequent travel, and base in Paris."

And sometimes, a woman made a critical decision to turn away from one career path and follow another, drawn by more interesting work, greater earning potential, or the possibility of having more time for her family. This woman's decision to leave teaching and enter a graduate program in a different discipline led to a long and very satisfying career:

> After three years into my teaching career, I realized that I was very unsatisfied by public high school and middle school teaching, and that, indeed, I was not particularly interested in teaching English at all. I had chosen an English major because I loved to read, not because I had any idea about research or critical scholarship ... I had learned of a museum studies program and it was as though a light bulb went off and I realized that for much of my life, objects were what resonated for me, and that I could potentially have a career working in museums if I went to this program.

In another case, a woman's career path took shape after she realized she would have to continue her education in order to find a job. "I enjoyed my major in college (psychology) but was concerned that there was not a way to earn a living unless I went into college teaching or clinical. Both required advanced degrees. I pursued the PhD almost as a matter of default."

I made the decision to put my family first.

Marlene, *lawyer and business partner*

Marlene's father and grandfather were both pharmacists. Her mother, who possessed a very strong work ethic, was actively involved in running the retail part of the family business, where Marlene, too, worked as a child and teenager. "It was understood I would go to college and have a career. My mother wanted me to become a stockbroker." Because her parents primarily focused their attention on making sure her brother became a doctor, Marlene said it was clear she would need to find a career. In high school, her mother took her to a vocational counselor who recommended she become a physical therapist. She was "scared" of science and chose economics as a major instead. While working in an office job at a mutual fund after college, Marlene became keenly aware that attorneys held the power and respect in the office, so she applied to law school. She was pregnant in her final year of law school when she made the decision to put her family first, by working either per diem or in her own practice. This decision led to a twenty-five-year partnership with other women, working primarily in family law. She found this arrangement enjoyable and helpful, even though she would have preferred a practice in real estate or tax. At the time of her interview, Marlene held an "of counsel" position with a small firm. She could control the number of clients she had, and her work was part-time, often conducted at a distance, allowing her to keep working when she and her husband relocated to a warmer climate in the winter. Marlene said she felt as though she were clinging to the past because she didn't have anything engaging or enjoyable enough to make her want to leave. She said she would like to make good use of her practical experiences in resolving problems, either through education or mediation. She loved teaching business law at a local teachers college and said her ideal situation would be "to wave a magic wand and become a college professor."

Whereas some women made early, decisive commitments that shaped their careers, others changed direction dramatically along the way. We found that midcareer coaching played an important role for some women in Cohort 25 by helping them to make a needed change and/or refocus their professional direction.

I bought myself a new career.

Savannah, *corporate executive in human resources and in sales, consultant*

Even though he had refused to allow his wife to work, Savannah's father, a bank executive, always assumed Savannah would have a career. For her mother, it was crucial that Savannah have opportunities she herself had been denied. She often referred to Savannah's future in terms of "when you have a career." In fact, at the time of her interview, Savannah described herself as having had three careers—in education, human resources, and consulting sales. With each new direction, she made an intentional, purposeful move. She began her career teaching handicapped preschool children, as part of an experimental, grant-based project. After two years she was promoted to a series of leadership roles within the childcare organization. Following changes in her personal life and a move to a new city, Savannah said she "bought herself" a new career through extensive assessment and career coaching. The insights she gained led to several strategic moves. She was recruited by headhunters and accepted a series of positions in Fortune 500 companies. Of one company in particular, she recalled that the corporate culture was very supportive of women; they were promoted and celebrated as "heroines" within the company. However, when the top leadership changed, everything changed, and in the new company culture, the women who had been celebrated were suddenly denigrated. Savannah had had a strong interest in the treatment of women all her life. She remembered that even at a young age, she had been appalled by many of the things she observed, such as the treatment of scantily clad waitresses and the objectification of women in general. Retired and working part-time as a consultant, Savannah facilitated programs for women in their twenties through their fifties, helping them develop their leadership skills. She was also looking for a way to make a contribution to the efforts against human trafficking.

DISCRIMINATION TAKES MANY FORMS

At the same time that there were expanding opportunities and challenging new career paths for women to follow, there were also road-blocks and detours along those paths. Just as there were colleagues who were helpful and supportive, there were also those who doubted women's abilities, saw them as threats or physical objects, or weren't interested in promoting or paying them equitably. In general, women talked about issues of discrimination quite matter-of-factly, but for some, looking back and reflecting on the workplace may have caused them to see inequities more sharply than in the past.

What was it like to be a woman in a workplace that was predominantly male? How did it affect individual women's careers? In answer to the question, "Was your organization male dominated?" two-thirds of the women answered yes. Conversely, less than a quarter of the women indicated that their organization was female dominated. Some women described the profession they entered as having a two-tiered system, delineated by gender. This was the case for two women who entered careers in higher education. One described the faculty at the time she began her career: "There were fifty-five men and five women in the college at the time I was hired. It was a male-dominated environment, without a lot of support for women." Another woman began her career in a university library: "Librarianship at that point was typically male led at the administrative level but heavily female at the middle management and front line level. This was changing in the late eighties and nineties."

"Did you encounter discrimination in your career?" Almost half the women in Cohort 25 answered yes. Others, without saying yes or no, indicated by their comments that they might not have been aware of discrimination, saying "probably" and "who knows, really." Of those who answered yes, the majority experienced discrimination based on gender. Other women, individually, said they had experienced discrimination based on race, marital status, health issues, professional rivalry, age, and nationality.

The effects and institutional responses to discrimination demonstrate how deeply the unfair treatment of women was engrained in workplace culture. One-third of the women said discrimination affected their salary; another third said their promotion or professional development was affected. When asked if they took action to address the discrimination they experienced, most women said no. When asked, "Did the organization take action to address the discrimination?" only two women said yes. Although one woman indicated her organization had twice taken action on her behalf, in general, women's comments demonstrated that institutional responses to discrimination could be both patronizing and slow in coming, as the comments from these two women made clear: "I called Personnel, hysterical. They called me back to say, 'We advise you not to sue.' I'd said nothing about suing, being too distraught to think" and "Late in my career the HR people felt I was underpaid relative to my peers."

Our questions about discrimination led to candid reflections about the culture of a workplace that, for some, was the setting for sexual harassment. One woman compared the undertone of condescension toward women to racism: "It's pervasive and always around." At the same time they were working to establish themselves and earn the respect of their male colleagues, women had to contend with unwanted sexual advances. "The head of my department put his hands on my hips one day and said, 'Some people have it and some don't, and you really have it.' "

Another woman described her experience traveling with a male colleague in her position as a national fundraiser:

> We would travel to fabulous places, and one evening with him and an Executive Vice President from a major international publication, the men were drunk and began hitting on me. Ten years later, watching the Anita Hill testimony, my mother said Hill must have egged Clarence Thomas on.[1] I told her I didn't know anyone who wasn't hit on by men she worked with.

As the following profile demonstrates, women could move up in professional rank, earn multiples degrees, be hired by international organizations, and continue to find sexual harassment ubiquitous in the workplace.

How fast can you type?

Harper, *international consultant, NGO leader, and business school administrator*

Harper thought having a "travel-bug" may have been inherited since her parents had traveled and worked abroad. When her career evolved to include a lot of travel, it became a plus and integral to her private and professional life. Whether to have a career was never a question; "it was what I and the women around me expected." Early interests drew Harper to her first career as a museum specialist, curator, and exhibits director. "From childhood, I loved museums, libraries, antiques and design, and discovered it was possible to have a career in those areas," though obstacles were sometimes discouraging. Indeed, applying for a junior manager post in an auction house, this Ivy Leaguer was told, "We don't interview girls for those jobs, but do you want to take a steno test?" This slight was not the only time Harper encountered discrimination in the workplace. Her striking appearance, while it sometimes won her favor, too often made her a target of sexual attention, stereotyping, and innuendo, especially as her name recalled that of a famous actress. As she described it, "In retrospect discrimination was a frequent, pervasive presence; I must have thought it was normal," and it was never an easy or fair fight. Harper's second, international career, influenced by her PhD and enabled by her MBA, began when she started her own consulting firm and moved to Europe with her husband. She spent several decades at a prominent international organization. She most enjoyed "working with key decision and policy makers, politicians and diplomats, being privy to cutting-edge aspects of policy, and orchestrating cooperative initiatives among representatives of government, business and industry, nongovernmental organizations, and academe." And, she added, "travel." Widowed for several years, Harper continued to go back and forth between the United States and Europe. She said she had to make a decision about where to set up another residence in the States—maybe someplace warm, because she was a swimmer—though the idea of restoring a historic property beckoned too.

Although discrimination in the workplace was pervasive, it was not going entirely unaddressed. In fact, the careers of some women were launched by institutional responses to gender-based discrimination, once the discrimination was uncovered by internal or external audits or through a lawsuit.

> Doing something professionally was how I found my sense of self.
> Paula, *corporate trainer and partner in organizational consulting firm*

Paula said she didn't recall having any discussions with her mother about a career, and her father framed Paula's career as "something to fall back on in case anything happens to your husband." Paula knew she wanted to earn a living and support herself. As she put it, she had a career long before she had a sense of self. In her heart of hearts, she wanted to be a psychologist, but without having any career guidance, and being, as she said, "clueless," she applied to a college that focused on experimental psychology rather than psychological counseling. When she discovered her mistake, she switched to a major in English, which she had always loved. After college, Paula was exposed to professional development opportunities that changed the direction of her career. She was first selected for a "Train the Trainer" program, established in response to a major discrimination lawsuit, and was later invited to participate in a program designed for women managers. Although the program was intended to develop women leaders, it helped Paula identify the career path she knew she wanted to follow: training and human resources for women. Paula joined an organizational consulting firm as a partner, and there she enjoyed the artistic aspects of designing the office space but found herself professionally growing further away from the coaching work she loved. She decided to take the advice she had often given others, to "take some time off." She cashed out of her partnership and took a sabbatical year for herself, during which she rented a potter's studio and traveled. After a year, Paula came to the decision that working for herself was the best option, so she began her own coaching practice, which she continued for almost two decades before joining an international career-management company. Paula said that as a young woman she had few role models, and years later, when the women's movement came into its own, she was aware of it only "in my peripheral vision." Even during the training programs she participated in early in her career, she didn't think of the connection to herself: "Perhaps that was because I saw the women's movement as philosophical, and what I was doing was very practical."

"YOU ALWAYS WONDER"

Although discrimination based on gender was most commonly identified by women in our study, women also pointed out other experiences in which discrimination played a role in their career opportunities. In reflecting on the influence of growing up in a predominantly black environment, a woman with broad executive experience said, "I have always been a person who was not taught to mistrust people. As a result, I bring out the 'race card' at the very last second." However, she said, she was not naive and knew people had ideas about "what people look like." She understood that people were judged by how they looked and spoke and the significance of first impressions. In referring to an opportunity she was denied early in her career, she said, "You always wonder why you don't get things when it seems you have equal qualifications . . . when there's no other explanation, you have to wonder."

Another pervasive and subtle form of discrimination women described was discrimination in opportunities. How often did women have jobs that involved a great deal of responsibility but in which they were offered limited opportunities, lower salaries, or less prestige than men? Women identified these positions in many ways: attorneys whose entire practice was in a less desirable niche area and academics whose advancement never reached the highest administrative roles. How often had it taken a number of years, or perhaps some distance, for them to realize what was happening? Did positions that felt like opportunities—strong, secure, and respected—obscure the fact that they were havens for women who worked harder and had fewer opportunities than men who moved up and around with greater ease in the same professions or institutions? As one woman put it, "There were 'huge gaps of omission' in opportunities for career development that could have come my way." Another pointed out the inequities in the type of work she was given:

> I was discriminated against in the sense of having limited opportunities —found that most men were happy to give their domestic relation cases to me and therefore my practice concentrated on family law ... I would have preferred to have practiced in real estate and tax, instead of having angry, complaining clients always in crisis.

Even when women recognized the places where their career opportunities or advancement might have been thwarted, overall, they talked about their careers with pride. Each woman seemed to have internalized a sense of responsibility for the professional path she followed. When things did not work out as she had planned, she turned and moved on. In the biography of Sally Ride, America's first woman in space, Lynn Sherr recalled Ms. Ride's ability to make strategic decisions and change direction in her career. An early instance of this occurred when she assessed her abilities and decided she did not have what it would take to become a tennis pro. She later said it was her forehand that kept her from a career in tennis, but as Sherr described it, "She also said, 'I realized finally and for certain, what I had realized but waffled on in the past: that my education, science, was more important to me than tennis was.' It wouldn't keep her from playing—and usually winning—over the next decade, but it would refocus her attention on physics. Sally pivoted and moved on."[2]

Similarly, the women of Cohort 25 knew how and when to *pivot* and move on. When one woman was told as a child that being a doctor was not an option for girls, she pivoted and earned a PhD instead, eventually creating her own very successful company. When another woman found herself in an academic appointment that felt stale and no longer stimulating, she employed her own "five-year rule," pivoted, and moved on to something much more challenging. The women in Cohort 25 refused to give up or to become cynical or resigned. When necessary, they changed direction and even changed their goals. Throughout their careers, they looked past obstacles and continued to move forward, adjusting and thriving regardless of the circumstances.

Table 3.1 Careers

Period of career interruption	68%
Period of restlessness during a job	68%
Job or role change as result of opportunities	80%
Opportunities as result of luck	60% said yes or somewhat
Career opportunities based on networking	92% said yes or sometimes
Found direction for fulfilling career	Before and after college and beginning with first job
What they enjoyed during the most satisfying and exciting period(s)	Creativity and problem solving Leadership, autonomy, and innovation Coaching, mentoring, teaching, and motivating staff Analyzing conditions Selling new ideas Deploying strategy to workforce Creating jobs for women Shattering stereotypes Hiring and on-boarding Being media spokesperson and making presentations Working with key decision and policy makers from governments, worldwide Organizing, executing, and achieving success of large, challenging projects Varied responsibilities and challenges Control over time and schedule Changing a culture and trying new, risky things Marketing and implementing brand strategies Technology immersion Customer satisfaction and making a difference in people's lives Travel
Worked in male-dominated organization	64%

Worked in female-dominated organization	20%
Experienced discrimination during career	56% said yes, and others said they might not have been aware
Took action to address discrimination	36% no
Organization took action to address discrimination	36% no
What they enjoyed most during job	72% creative challenges 60% working with others 52% professional recognition

NOTES

1. During 1991 hearings on the appointment of Clarence Thomas to the Supreme Court, Anita Hill's testimony that he sexually harassed her at the Department of Education and the Equal Employment Opportunity Commission drew public attention to the issue of workplace sexual harassment in the United States. Shortly after the hearings, Congress passed a law giving victims of sexual harassment the right to seek damage awards, back pay, and reinstatement.

2. Lynn Sherr, *Sally Ride: America's First Woman in Space* (New York: Simon & Schuster, 2014), 39–40.

4

At the Point of Transition: Individual Strengths and Concerns

The ability of Baby Boomer professional women to *pivot* had never been as important as it was when they looked ahead to the transition to retirement. They had reached the point where it may have seemed as though the critical components of their lives—not only career but also family and identity—had become entirely unsettled. Many women in Cohort 25 spoke of the turmoil that accompanied the transitional period leading up to and following their decision to leave their full-time careers. What to do next, what to expect, where to place their energy—these questions were very much on their minds. Eventually, they shifted and pivoted more than once as they sorted out their next steps.

They were going through a complex, multilayered transition process, saying good-bye to the decades-long identity and demands of a career. They were also realizing and accepting that aging and health issues would play a bigger role in the next phase of their lives. The range of emotions the women were experiencing was complex and different for each person. The process itself was not linear or tidy; at times, in interviews and conversations, women contradicted themselves. They spoke openly about their ambivalence and uncertainty. As we will see, the women in Cohort 25 moved through this period of personal uncertainty to reach a new stage of greater confidence and happiness about the future. But in this chapter, we are trying to capture how they saw themselves and what concerned them about retirement at the time of their interviews.

Because the women of Cohort 25 were positioned at various points along the continuum of their career transition when we first met them, we were able to collect twenty-five individual perspectives on that transition. To learn more about how they saw themselves in this admittedly complicated period, we asked them about their employment status, what they had enjoyed most about their careers, what they saw as their strengths, what they hoped to do and have going forward, and what concerned them. In addition to providing us with important collective insights about Cohort 25, responding to these questions had a benefit for the women themselves. It offered them the opportunity to reflect on and verbalize things they felt very strongly about, from positive experiences of the past to the hopes and fears they held for the future.

ARE YOU STILL WORKING?

First, to develop a snapshot of their employment status at the time of their interviews, we gave the women of Cohort 25 a simple checklist to complete. However, the responses were far from simple. During the eight-month period when we were conducting personal interviews, several women were straddling the line separating their full-time career and retirement. In many cases, the line was not sharply delineated: Some women had taken early retirement in their fifties; others were shifting from full-time to part-time employment; some had retired but continued to work part-time; others were still working full-time in their mid-to-late sixties. At the time of their interviews, the majority of the women were age sixty-five and older. Almost one-third were still working full-time.

These sample responses, arranged by profession and age of the Cohort 25 respondents, make it clear that drawing a correlation between age and professional employment status is problematic:

Working part-time, considering retiring in one to two years.

Business Owner, age 60

Retired early over five years ago.

Lawyer, age 62

Working part-time, retired within last three to four years.

Journalist, age 64

Retired, not looking for employment but continually thinking about it.

NGO Leader, age 66

Working full-time, considering retiring in one to two years.

Interior Designer, age 68

When we add the number of women still working full-time to the total number of women working part-time, both retired and nonretired, we find that, all together, 64 percent of the women were still in the workforce in some capacity.

At the same time, many women were engaged in other activities outside the workplace. One-third were serving on nonprofit boards; a few were mentoring or tutoring. A remarkable 84 percent were looking for new opportunities, whether volunteer, personal, or professional.

WHAT DID YOU ENJOY MOST IN YOUR CAREER?

To understand how women felt about and were affected by their careers as they approached retirement, we asked them to tell us about the things they had enjoyed. Some of the most enthusiastic and detailed responses to our survey came in answer to the open-ended question: "What did you enjoy about your job during the most satisfying and exciting periods of your career?"

The women in Cohort 25 were obviously very happy to be asked this question. When we collated their answers, we found they could be sorted into three key areas, all describing what the women valued and found satisfying in their careers: creative challenges, working with others, and professional recognition. The responses to this question were so consistently powerful, and so frequently aligned along similar themes, that we decided to include virtually all of them.

Creative Challenges

In talking about what they enjoyed about their jobs, women enthusiastically described the challenges they took on, both within their careers and within the organizations where they worked. Some women vividly recalled the enjoyment they found in the intellectual challenges of problem solving, critical thinking, and analysis, whether their careers were spent in education or in the corporate world, as we heard in the following responses. From a teacher: "I enjoyed the varied responsibilities. Each year brought new unexpected challenges." From a psychologist/executive coach: "The ability to change the culture, make an impact, and the opportunity to try new and risky things." And from an executive recruiting professional: "I was encouraged to think—to analyze conditions, think through problems, and to solve them within a supportive environment."

Sometimes, being able to create something new—whether curricula, jobs, or museum exhibits—was the most satisfying part of a career. Again, the following selection of responses revealed a remarkable consistency. From a scientist in an international corporation: "I enjoyed being supported to create a long term idea." From a science teacher/ technology specialist: "Working with teachers, spending time with students, creating new and exciting ways to teach science and motivate staff and students." From an entrepreneur: "Creating jobs for women and shattering stereotypes while solving challenging business problems." And from two university administrators: "Loved the creativity, loved the problem solving, enjoyed leading people by letting them be creative," and, simply, "being creative and working with people."

Long before Anita Hill's 1991 testimony in the Clarence Thomas Supreme Court confirmation hearings, one of the women in our study was already working in the area of sexual harassment, as an administrator for a large university. In her words, the work was "fascinating and creative ... Not the happiest subject matter, but a very creative time." Another woman recounted the pleasure of the creativity she experienced while working in a gifted education program. She won a grant for a unit she wrote on architecture, combining math, science, and engineering components. She taught the unit for years and kept in touch with some of her students who, years later at forty-five to fifty years old, still remembered walking the streets with her as fourth graders, studying the buildings in their historic city.

For an art museum curator, opening the museum's collection to a wider audience provided the greatest creative challenge and satisfaction:

> I enjoyed presenting the art to the public and giving them opportunities to be enriched by the art. I treasured the time that I spent doing research, so that the fullest possible story could be told. I spent many satisfying hours writing labels and authoring publications. In my final years [at the gallery], I was thrilled to participate in [an open-air sculpture park project] which opened up the gallery to the community in perpetuity. I delighted in seeing people come onto the grounds, particularly children and visitors who I knew would never have felt welcome had we not taken down the fence and installed inviting opportunities to engage with art.

Other women found their work most satisfying and exciting when the challenge involved convincing others to support a new idea. A corporate operations professional was enthusiastic about "the challenges of organizing large projects, executing an action plan, and achieving success within time restraints," and a corporate executive spoke of several projects that illustrated the evolution of her career: "I enjoyed selling new ideas on how to do things in the workplace, new ways to assess handicapped children, new ways to design manufacturing work, new ways to deploy strategy to the workforce."

Working with Others

Many times, the women in Cohort 25 referred to the enjoyment and satisfaction they experienced while working with others in a professional setting, whether that entailed building a successful team or developing relationships with clients, students, or colleagues. These responses often came from women who held significant leadership positions in corporations and in businesses, international agencies, and universities. Their educational backgrounds, ranging from degrees in law and science to library studies and international finance, were as varied as their positions; but the deep connection between collaboration and personal satisfaction was enforced repeatedly, across the professions, as we can hear in their responses. From a scientist: "I have always been a dreamer and continue to see possibilities. The more I learn, the more I imagine and I try to involve others in creating that possibility." From a lawyer: "Joining industry organizations and being active with them." From an international consultant: "Working with key decision and policy makers from many governments, worldwide." And from a university administrator: "Working with many different groups of people, including hundreds of students on big and small initiatives."

A career consultant was happiest when she went to work at a large career management firm that shared her goals and values:

> I loved working with a group of smart, energetic people. Everyone clicked; all had the goal of being successful and dynamic. The members of the group liked each other and held each other in mutual respect.

As she described it, despite the fact that the expectations for that particular office had been low at first, the group was extremely successful in working together: "We watched each other work with clients—everyone was gracious. We had shared values."

And sometimes, the pleasure of working with others took the form of directly assisting them, as three women described. From a human resources professional: "I enjoyed helping people make career decisions." From a corporate business leader: "Serving our clients in a very special and moving way after 9/11." And from a partner in a consulting firm: "Guiding people through a difficult transition in their careers; helping them to regain confidence and make good career choices."

Professional Recognition

The third category we identified in women's answers to the question about what they enjoyed most had to do with the opportunities and recognition that accompanied professional advancement. For some women in Cohort 25, opportunities for leadership were defining factors in what they enjoyed about their careers. Two women who had spent their careers working for large institutions listed leadership among several other aspects of their work that they had enjoyed. The first woman had spent years managing complex, high-level projects at a university: "I enjoyed autonomy, leadership, innovation, creation." The second worked for a major international organization, where she also wore many hats. She said she most enjoyed "teamwork, technology immersion, project management and leadership opportunities."

For others, enjoyment of professional recognition was described in terms of having a positive reputation or being called upon to represent their organization. Specific examples included being well known and well liked by the corporate office, having a strong reputation in the industry, being the media spokesperson for the company, being invited to speak on many panels, and running a top-performing office and receiving recognition for that.

Professional recognition also took the form of having significant access or influence, as described here by a lawyer, a corporate business leader, and an international consultant: "I enjoyed knowing amazing people who worked for iconic organizations"; "being privy to cutting edge aspects of policy issues"; and "successfully orchestrating intergovernmental coordination, while bringing in business and industry, NGOs, and academe."

From the range of responses to this question, we can distill key elements regarding what the women of Cohort 25 enjoyed most in their careers. The excitement and sense of accomplishment they described is essentially *the ability to be creatively engaged and recognized in widely diverse settings*. The engagement that characterized their careers is a distinguishing feature of this generation of women professionals. Although they were sometimes the first member of their family to complete college and often the first to have a professional career, the opportunities that opened up for the women of Cohort

25, combined with their education and eagerness to move forward, made them great team players, even if they hadn't been able to benefit from Title IX. Their childhoods and early career experiences were often shaped by male authority figures, and they had very few examples of female achievement; nonetheless, these women went on to become leaders in their fields. They took on and were given increasing levels of responsibility. They came up with new ideas and new approaches. They put together successful, efficient teams. They were excited by being recognized for their expertise, leadership, and success.

WHAT INFLUENCED YOUR DECISION TO LEAVE YOUR CAREER?

As much as the women of Cohort 25 loved and flourished in their careers, at the point when we met them, many were grappling with the decision of when to stop working. Some had already left their careers, but others anticipated working for several more years. Without a set mandatory retirement age, the decision to leave a career may be affected by countless factors beyond the calendar. We tried to zero in on the issues, both workplace and personal, that might precipitate that decision. (See Table 4.1: Leaving the Workplace.) We asked women, "Are/Were there issues at the end of your current career that influenced your staying or leaving?" Two-thirds of them said yes.

To follow up, we asked, "Are any of the following representative of those issues?" When given a checklist, 20 percent of the women cited decisions of a new or changing management/organization; when the figures were combined, another 20 percent indicated that their work was becoming more boring and less meaningful, and they were experiencing burnout.

The number of individuals who selected each descriptor was fairly small, but in their open-ended comments, women provided much more detail about what they experienced as they approached the end of their careers. In some cases, changes in their family circumstances were the impetus for reevaluating their work lives. The change sometimes came from their children, when the children's families expanded and relocated, as this woman noted, "Not really issues, but life changes coming down the road—children living at a distance, grandchildren—I knew that I wanted to step off the constricted, schedule-driven treadmill." Another woman, who was still working full-time, captured in a few words what she was facing at the end of her career: "Energy level—needing to help ninety-five-year-old mother and help with grandchildren, desire to get back to creating art."

Some women whose careers were spent in the corporate world wrote about the effects of feeling diminished or marginalized in the workplace toward the end of those careers. They described being given lesser responsibilities before retirement, being ignored, or knowing their skills were being underutilized. For people who had moved successfully through the ranks, who were recruited and promoted because of their expertise, it was especially demoralizing to have that expertise ignored and to be sidelined at the culmination of their careers, as recounted in this example from a corporate operations professional:

> The younger generation re-inventing the wheel became routine and boring. Input from individuals who held responsibilities for numerous years was looked at as old school and we were seen as ready to be put out to pasture.

Changes in a profession—in the nature of the work and in the personal toll it extracted—were often cited in women's decisions to retire. This was especially true for these two educators: "The field of education drastically changed over the years. By the end of my career, I was walking through the days without the enthusiasm I once had" and "Terrible understaffing, with eighty–to–one hundred-hour work weeks."

Some women were just plain tired of how they had been treated by those in the top tiers of leadership, citing "highly incompetent leaders in the organization." As one woman in higher education put it, "I was too successful and good at what I did to put up with it again."

Changes in the workplace, dwindling opportunities, and sometimes, even the painful loss of colleagues were all mentioned in the decision to retire: "The shows where I exhibited and sold my artwork are slowing down; I am slowing down. The traveling and physical work without the rush is draining" and "People that I worked closely with had either died or retired. I also had to do some retooling and I did not have a lot of energy for that."

Financial concerns can also be extremely important in a woman's decision about when to leave a full-time career or when to shift to a transitional career plan. However, numerous other, less quantifiable factors, both psychological and personal, affected individual decisions about when the time was right to move on. For some women in Cohort 25, what they could expect from the future was much less clear and less predictable than it had been during the years when they were rising through the ranks professionally, looking forward to promotions or new opportunities. Factors such as downsizing or reorganization within a company sometimes had an effect on their decision, as did personal factors, including changes in health or family circumstances.

Sometimes, the decision to move on came unexpectedly, with the suddenness of a revelation. One woman from Cohort 25, a sales professional and entrepreneur, so much enjoyed working on her late-career MBA that it became hard for her to focus on her work after that. She began to consider making a dramatic change. "Everything I did required travel. I couldn't stand the travel, didn't need the money." After realizing how burned out she had become, she made the decision to sell her company and pursue other opportunities. She described her realization that it was time to move on by comparing it to the seek-and-find challenge in a popular children's book: "It's like *Where's Waldo?*—once you see it, you can't *not* see it."

Not everyone had a *"Where's Waldo?* moment" in which the vision of a new future suddenly appeared: sharp and irrefutable. Instead, the shift to the next stage might have involved many incremental steps. We asked, "Is it possible to make a slow, gradual move from a full-time career to the next stage?" For some women, the answer was yes, *sometimes*. Two women from Cohort 25, one a corporate lawyer and business leader and the other a university administrator, gave very different and candid responses to the question of timing. In each case, the prospect of exciting new work supplanted thoughts of retirement:

> We have a lot of business coming in from clients and I don't want to walk away; I had planned to retire a year ago, but now will continue working. I would like to try something new, so would leave for that reason if and when I do.
>
> I have children at home under twenty years old. So, while retiring is attractive because I am getting older at this point, I'm not 100% comfortable without some kind of income stream. It doesn't have to be the same level because I do have retirement savings, but something I would be more comfortable with, something rather than nothing. Also, and this is as much a factor as the money issue at this point, I see lots of possibilities with the work I am doing for next few years. I can see continuing to make a contribution doing this in my current capacity, or perhaps, if an opportunity arises to do something else, not full time, but that uses my skill set and engages me creatively, that could push me in another direction. This is why I am somewhat ambivalent about when to retire.

At other times, though, the decision to retire was driven by outside events or responsibilities. Then, rather than controlling the timing, a woman had to react to changes beyond her control. One woman faced immediate demands for caregiving when her husband suddenly became disabled. Others dealt with or were anticipating the imminent needs of their aging parents. This woman retired immediately after her father's death, knowing how her own circumstances were about to change: "My father passed away in 2007 and I knew I would have more responsibility assisting my mother who lived in Pennsylvania. Within a year she moved to the city where I live."

Or, it might have been the realization that things *could* change that drove a woman's decision to leave her full-time career. A woman who described herself as being in "phase three" of her life," what she referred to as the "selfish me phase," recognized the fragility of her situation when she retired. Her eighty-seven-year-old mother lived in Florida, and if her mother's health declined, she could foresee moving her up north. For the time being, she said she wanted to enjoy everything she could.

Unless the decision to retire was made suddenly, for personal or other reasons, it is likely that the transition to retirement would take months or years. The entire process of preparing for and anticipating retirement and eventually moving from working full-time to being fully retired from a career could, in fact, take many years. Although it is impossible to set up clear lines of demarcation between working and not working, we wanted to capture the feelings and concerns women in Cohort 25 were experiencing at the point when we met them and when most of them were thinking about or had recently entered the process of transition from their full-time careers. To do this, we posed a series of questions.

A PERSONAL INVENTORY AT THE POINT OF TRANSITION

"What are your strengths?" When we asked the women of Cohort 25 to select from a list of adjectives that described their strengths at the point of their career transition, the traits of being self-reliant, acting independently, supporting others, and understanding people and situations intuitively were ranked very highly. By contrast, less than half chose nurturing, being a team player, or seeking consensus as one of their strengths.

Interestingly, as they assessed their strengths at the point of transition, the women of Cohort 25 were more likely to choose personal qualities of self-reliance and independence than qualities that served them well in the workplace, such as being a team player or seeking consensus. It seems very possible that at the same time they were approaching this major professional transition, they were also approaching another, more personal transition, in which they were thinking carefully about who they were and what essential strengths they would need to bring to the next stage of their lives.

When the women added other strengths they considered personally important to them, they listed characteristics that transcended the workplace. These included the empathy implied in "being kind and wise" and the tenacity of "perseverance and vision." At the same time, some respondents unequivocally stressed their management or leadership strengths, making it clear they still had both the desire and the ability to take on challenges and put their expertise and skills to use.

Collectively, these responses offered many different, even contradictory, impressions. They created a portrait of Cohort 25 as women who saw themselves as very independent and confident in their abilities. As much as they enjoyed working with others during their careers, when they assessed their strengths at the point when they were moving on from those careers, they ranked traits that involved dealing directly with others *lower* than those that involved acting on their own. The importance they placed on independence and self-reliance harked back to the women's descriptions of themselves when they were young. When they looked to the future, to their lives and identities beyond the professions or institutions, they saw many of the same fundamental character traits as their most important strengths.

The importance of personal values in women's lives and careers came up several times in their individual comments. When women added words of their own to describe their strengths, many of the descriptors referred to their values. Not only were their strengths based in values, but those values were also consistently described in terms of others, as in these examples: "inspiring others to improve/save lives," "motivating others to act to further a cause," and "being kind and wise."

Even the nature of the work they engaged in brought a kind of spiritual satisfaction to some women. As a museum curator observed, "Working with an object that has come from the soul of another human being is almost a sacred thing." Talking about work and talking about values were sometimes synonymous. For example, when describing the difference she made in people's lives, one woman said her role "took into account teaching, nurturing, and unconditional love." When asked how she defined herself, a customer service professional wove together personal and practical qualities: "I am very kind. I embrace a situation and people and am an organized professional."

The nature of the language women used to describe their strengths emphasizes a quality we see again and again. Women's sense of themselves, their roles, and even their accomplishments are *relational*, a quality that is vital as we talk about making a plan for the future.

What Activities Are You Interested In?

To develop a better understanding of what the women in Cohort 25 were interested in outside their working lives, we asked them to list activities they were serious about pursuing or to which they had already committed. The comments of three women—an attorney, an arts consultant, and a teacher—revealed their enthusiasm and drive, not only for getting new projects off the ground but also for seeing them through: "I would like to work with vulnerable animals; run a shelter or sanctuary; volunteer or get something started in this area"; "I am working on a very creative project—a ground-breaking television documentary—and my most recent book will be published this summer. Both involve significant writing and research"; and "I'm involved with a philanthropic endeavor, where 100 women invested $1,000 each to give away for a particular project. Projects are chosen based on grants submitted each year. They are all expertly written and hard to whittle down. I like this model of collective giving: All the money goes where the group chooses. And the women are all very bright; all ages, religions, races; all terrific."

Other women identified more general areas where they were considering or had already begun to focus their passions: women's issues, anti-Semitism, human trafficking. Several women told us they had writing projects in mind: some were deeply personal pieces; others were significant research works. One woman had been encouraged to write a guide to parenting; another envisioned a comic novel about her experiences in health care. While some were looking forward to having the time to write the book they had long imagined, others talked more about the value of writing itself. Rather than committing to a large postretirement project, they wanted to use written language as a way to reflect on their own experiences. This woman, a lawyer who had worked as a professional writer both during her full-time career and afterward, talked about turning to the more personal genre of memoir. She had thought hard about how she would allocate her time in order to make this possible: "For the past five years, I have been doing part-time freelance writing and was on several nonprofit boards. I am phasing into less time on volunteer commitments and more time for my own pursuits, such as writing classes and yoga."

Any Unfinished Business?

When we asked, "Do you look back at things you didn't do and wonder if you could do them now?" the responses were split virtually fifty-fifty. For some, the question stimulated thoughts of accomplishments and recognition a woman might have felt she had missed: "run a marathon," "attend a Seven Sisters College," or "run for elective office." In other instances, the responses revealed a desire to have more private time, to get away, pursue personal interests, and rest. One woman's response covered just about everything: "Road trips, advanced painting, sleeping, not having to take decisions, plan etc."

Despite the fact that they had been very successful in their careers, many women listed higher academic or professional goals among the things they would like to do. These included "get an MBA," "become an administrator," and "teach at a university or even community college."

Some women were slightly curious about paths they hadn't taken, but they were content, overall, with the decisions they had made. These two women reflected briefly on the paths they had chosen *not* to follow—pursuing an advanced and delaying marriage:

> Missed opportunities, or more aptly, roads not taken, are not available now. I used to regret not pursuing a medical degree, but lost that desire when my husband was ill. However, I have a yen to have a law degree (but less to do one), so that I could counsel on retirement and estate planning, including legal aspects.
>
> If I had not gotten married when I did, would I have been further along in my career at the time? But getting married and moving to places we did impacted my life and career and afforded me greater opportunities.

We asked the women of Cohort 25 to tell us more about themselves at the point when they were considering their career transition. (See Table 4.2: Next Steps.) "Which of the following are important to you now?" Much like a personal to-do list, the checklist included activities that addressed a range of issues.

What Do You Need to Have?

Having a social network, staying current, spending time with younger people, and having professional recognition and status were identified as important by over half the women. Being patient with the process of transition, joining a book club, recentering themselves, and finding their place/identity were important to roughly one-third of the women. They ranked having structure and a regular schedule only slightly higher than having a place and people to talk to about the process of transition or prioritizing.

At the time we met them, when they were each thinking about the transition after their careers, the women of Cohort 25 were adamant: they wanted to be active and stay involved with others. That included, especially, people who were younger. Not content to inhabit a retiree-only environment, they wanted a diverse social network.

Our survey did not explicitly address the more intangible qualities women may have been searching for, but in answer to "Which of the following are important to you now?" one woman answered in capital letters and pointedly added a new category to the list we had provided: "Need to have: *a sense of purpose*." Another went further, elaborating on the need for spiritual awareness and the importance of including it in the list:

> The survey does not cover the area of spiritual awareness and wisdom development as either a need or a driver of one's personal commitment to the work we do following retirement. I strongly feel that we focus on areas that we feel passionate about in terms of need for change, understanding and, most importantly, compassion.

When we asked this same scientist to say more about her thoughts on spirituality and wisdom development, she talked about women reaching the age fifty-five or so, having taken care of their family and career, and now asking "What do I want to do?" and "What *did* I want to do?" She continued:

> Is there a road not taken that you still want to experience? Are you beginning to experience that road? The wisdom part comes from choices. You know what things really encourage your heart, not your head. Is the wisdom you developed allowing you to pursue this? The heart can be synonymous with the soul. Is it bringing you a sense of peace and calmness? The peace you let go in those previous fifty-five years?

They may have set aside hopes for earning another advanced degree or running a marathon, but when women talked about their lives, they often spoke of other kinds of aspirations, some perhaps more difficult to fulfill or document. These were aspirations based on individual values, often seen as fundamental to a life where busyness is no longer a dominating force.

What Do You Need to Do?

Exercise, both intellectual and physical, was of high importance. Over three-quarters of the women indicated that keeping their minds active and challenged and exercising regularly are priorities. During their interviews, many of the women again emphasized their commitment to exercise, saying they regularly scheduled physical activity, whether through a daily swim, weekly riding lessons, or regular yoga retreats. Others made time for golf, kayaking, and horseback riding.

How Important Is Supplemental Income?

To determine whether women's drive to keep working full-time beyond their traditional retirement age or working part-time after retirement was driven by financial concerns, we asked them about the importance of earning supplemental income. A total of 40 percent of the women indicated that supplemental income was either somewhat or very important, but at least one person made the distinction between needing income for financial reasons and needing it for psychological reasons. As she put it, earning supplemental income is "somewhat important, psychologically, but not really needed." Her statement reminds us of just how significant it was for women to achieve independence, financial and otherwise, through their careers. Within that context, it is easy to understand the psychological importance of continuing to earn money.

SHIFTING THE EMPHASIS FROM NEEDS TO WANTS

We shifted the emphasis from needs to wants when we asked, "What do you want to do?" When we asked women to indicate which activities on a checklist they would like to pursue, the numbers were very high for travel, spending time with family, and creative projects. Given the time constraints and level of responsibility of many of their careers, it is not surprising that the women were looking forward to activities that might have been difficult to arrange or for which they had only limited time in the past.

Women in Cohort 25, like many other professional women Baby Boomers, were entering a phase of their lives in which they were free to identify what it was they would like to do, whether it was spending time with children and family, traveling without a fixed itinerary, or being able to engage in creative work without deadlines or interruptions. However, as the responses below suggested, at the time of their interviews, many of the women in Cohort 25 were still sorting out what it would take to make this new phase a reality.

What, If Anything, Stands in the Way of Your Doing These Things?

Asked about the impediments or obstacles that kept them from engaging in the things they would like to do, just over half of the women said there was *nothing* standing in the way. When the responses indicating financial, time, and health constraints as obstacles were added together, the total was fewer than the number of responses that indicated nothing was standing in the way of the women's engaging in the things they would like to do. However, when asked to comment on other factors, several women indicated that family responsibilities played a role in how free they were to take on other activities. Even though she was still working, this woman's husband was retired and eager to play golf year-round. The tug of their bicoastal attachments was very strong:

> My husband wants to be in a warm climate for the winter so I am not in my home area for four months of the year. I also want to be available to spend time with my young grandchildren who live both near my home and also on the West Coast. I don't feel that I am in any one place long enough to make a commitment to a long- term project.

This woman was not alone. For decades, women balanced family and work during their careers. They became experts in making the shifts in scheduling and attention that were required to keep the parts of their lives running smoothly, and in many cases, they were still doing just that as they approached retirement. However, they were also rich in experience and knowledgeable about resources, and even with the obstacles they described, women anticipated being able to engage in many activities during the next stage of their lives. What, then, were their concerns at the point of transition?

What Are Your Concerns?

In response to this question, over half of the women in Cohort 25 indicated that they were concerned about becoming isolated and experiencing ill health. Their other significant concerns included falling behind in technology, responsibility for others, loss of relationships, and their financial future.

Additional comments from Cohort 25 illustrated the wavering boundary between present and future concerns. At the same moment when they were preparing to leave their careers, perhaps looking back and assessing their professional lives, women were also looking straight ahead, knowing their lives could change at any moment. Their concerns were sometimes deeply personal, as we heard in this woman's words: "I am concerned about a loss of relationship: My closest relationship is about to change, as he is ill."

Concern about possible or impending changes echoed through the response of this woman who was recently retired but immersed in a volunteer project that had grown out of her professional work:

> I don't have any health concerns currently, but am only too aware that that can change on a dime and it makes me anxious to think of not being able to complete or at least launch the work that is important to me. ... As new grandparents, I think that at least one of my kids has an expectation that I will be very available to help care for the baby (which I had offered to do) but it will involve travel and time away from the project I'm working on ... so considering how that will be balanced.

Among the many changes Cohort 25 women were making in retirement, one we heard often was a new focus on activities related to their home and family. While they were often extremely gratifying, these activities—from nurturing grandchildren to overseeing the building of a new home—reflected a dramatic shift in how and where women directed their energies and abilities. This new focus could also create new concerns, as we heard in comments suggesting the women were sometimes wary, even afraid, of slipping into the traditional roles they had observed in their mothers' and grandmothers' lives. A retired entrepreneur described her apprehension with these words: "We have had big, bold lives, and now we find ourselves almost in a housewife role."

HAVING ENOUGH TIME

At the culmination of demanding careers, the women of Cohort 25 had unquestionably earned the right to set aside time for themselves. Some women referred to "hoarding" time for their own pursuits, setting limits on how much time they were willing to devote to caring for their grandchildren, and enjoying independence "while I can," knowing that their aging parents could soon need more attention. Their language revealed a difficult, even painful, sense of time as a fleeting commodity that could easily be lost to the needs of others, even those, especially those, whom they loved the most.

There was also another quality to these words, one that was subtler, as women struggled to keep a firm grip on time for themselves by setting limits, saying "no." What women sometimes referred to as "selfishness" in the use of their time, when they spoke about "doing things for me" or setting aside "time for me," may in fact have been an acknowledgment of the emotional toll of caregiving. Although most of them described their caregiving responsibilities as part-time, still 40 percent of the women in Cohort 25 were taking care of others in some capacity.

CAREGIVING FOR THREE, SOMETIMES FOUR, GENERATIONS

With the resources and time to help their children and nurture their grandchildren, women were often very involved in the lives of the next two generations. They were caring for infants and toddlers and closely following school projects, social events, and sports activities of older children. For women who may not have had the time or career flexibility to spend as much time as they would have liked with their own children, being active, hands-on grandmothers offered a welcomed new opportunity.

Other women assumed a great deal of decision making as well as care for their elderly parents, often changing their own lives in significant ways, such as taking an immediate retirement or arranging to be available for regular transatlantic trips to care for ailing relatives.

If they were not already actively involved in caregiving, many women anticipated that it would become a major responsibility for them and that the needs of others would be critical to plans they made for the future. As one woman said, "My wife is a full-time homemaker. However, she has a life-threatening illness, so our situation can change at any time."

The caregiving needs they described could be enormous, requiring financial and emotional resources as well as time and attention. Sometimes they found caring for others to be exhilarating, even comforting. But it could also be frustrating and exhausting, with little respite. A woman whose husband experienced a serious disability described caregiving this way: "Caring for an infirm spouse/parent is not the same as getting a child off to day care. It's almost like having an infant."

How did women attend to the needs of others while continuing to pursue their own interests and goals? This may very well have been one of the biggest challenges for Baby Boomer professional women in general as they left the workplace. Just at the time when they were making the transition to life after a full-time career, in many cases, the needs of others were growing dramatically and unexpectedly.

Table 4.1   Leaving the Workplace

Were there issues that influenced their staying in or leaving their career	68% yes
Issues that were basis of decision	20% new or changing management 12% burnout 8% work became more boring and less meaningful Other: 16% energy level 12% transition to consulting 4% care for parents 4% relocation
Adjectives best describing strengths	92% being self-reliant 84% acting independently 80% supporting others 80% understanding people and situations intuitively 72% building relationships 68% providing direction 60% willing to take risks 48% being a team player 48% nurturing 36% seeking consensus
Work status	32% work full-time 16% work part-time 16% retired and work part-time 36% retired
Volunteer	32% nonprofit board 12% mentor 4% tutor 16% other
Looking for new opportunities	20% professional 28% personal 36% volunteer
Part-time and full-time caregiving	36% part-time 4% full-time

Table 4.2   Next Steps

What is important now: need to have	60% social network 52% professional recognition/status 28% structure/regular schedule 24% place/people to talk about and think through the process of transition
What is important now: need to do	84% keep mind active and challenged 76% exercise regularly 60% stay current 56% spend time with younger people 36% join a book club 36% recenter 36% find place/identity 32% be patient with transition process 24% prioritize
What they want to do at this point in life	92% travel 88% spend time with family 72% do creative projects 44% write 28% research
What stands in the way	52% nothing 28% time constraints 12% financial constraints 4% health issues 16% other: family 4% no response
Need for supplemental income	60% not important 32% somewhat important 8% very important
Concerns	52% becoming isolated 52% experiencing ill health 40% falling behind in technology 40% responsibility for others 36% loss of relationships 28% financial future
Reasons for agreeing to be part of this project	Engage with a group of their peers Share their experiences Hear others' experiences See what others are doing and feeling Be part of a group that is strategizing and problem solving this phase Engage in personal reflection Gain insight to make this next phase more satisfying

The broad parameters of Cohort 25—birth years and professional status—certainly helped us identify a diverse and representative group of Baby Boomer women. Nonetheless, their individual lives could only be suggested, but not contained, in any generalizations about the group. What we do know is that at the time when we were first getting to know them, they were moving out of the workplace in a manner that was consistent with how they had spent their working lives. They were paying attention to and giving credit for the things they had enjoyed in their careers; they were seeing their self-reliance and independence as strengths. They were articulate about what they were aspiring to and what concerned them. They were sorting things out and getting ready for the next big step.

5

The Confidence of a Cohort

During the period between their interviews with us and when they met one another in the focus groups, the women of Cohort 25 had plenty of time for self-reflection. In the focus groups, the introspection and analysis they had engaged in during and after their interviews found full expression. They opened up, encouraged one another, and easily acknowledged how much they welcomed the opportunity to talk with each other. In apparent contrast to the responses from the surveys, when the women met in the focus groups, the feelings they expressed about the need to talk to others were very different. In that context, among other professionals facing similar challenges, the women were emphatic and unanimous in their desire to seek out further opportunities for conversations with their peers.

A strong collective identity emerged from the Cohort 25 focus groups. The women recognized in each other's experiences common themes and triumphs as well as mutual concerns. As the attention shifted from the experience of individual women to that of a group, the women's voices changed, too. "I" became "we," and with that shift, women immediately realized, or were reminded of, the strength of a group identity. Processing ideas and recording their thoughts, they were enthusiastic and eager to talk with one another and, ultimately, with others beyond their groups. Concerns that had left them individually feeling uncertain about the future immediately turned into connections when they met other women of a similar age and with experiences like their own.

ADVICE FROM FOCUS GROUPS

We were very pleased by the way the women of Cohort 25 opened up and added new dimensions to the focus groups. They discovered greater nuance in the questions we posed, enriched the conversations with personal stories, and raised provocative points

we had not considered. For example, a conversation about the timing of one's decision to leave a career took off in new directions
when the women in a focus group added a new element by saying
one's personal career focus could diminish, just as much as one's
psychic or physical energy. To help other Baby Boomer women professionals consider this possibility, they suggested questions for
those who were contemplating whether to stay in or leave their
careers:

> How do changes affect you?
>   Do you still love it?
>   Do you want to continue or are you tired of what you are doing?

Straightforward and delivered as if from colleague to colleague,
these questions were intended to be helpful to other women. The language itself reached out to others, drawing them into a conversation.
The repeated use of the word "you" resounded as the women spoke
directly to their peers: "Think about yourself, what you are experiencing, and what you want."

In addition to posing these questions, women in a focus group
advised others to "give time for reflecting and leisure, time to decide,
rather than going from something to something." This advice emphasized a deliberate slowing down, taking time to allow for the reflection
and contemplation that may be required when making the decision to
leave a career. What many women discovered is that this process is not
quick. Some deliberately gave themselves a year of "saying no" without taking on any new commitments. Others found that devoting a
year to the process was just the beginning. As we will see, the process
of self-reflection and clarifying what was important was an evolving
one and might, in fact, go on for years.

MOVING PAST TITLES AND LABELS

After decades of striving to move ahead, to attain new positions and
embrace wider areas of responsibility, women in Cohort 25 had
become accustomed to what some of them referred to as the "labels"
that embodied their professional lives. Those labels—the positions or
titles and all the credentials, experience, and authority they conveyed
—were hard to give up. What exactly would be lost when the labels
were left behind? What would take their place? Sharing their thoughts
in a focus group, women made a list of the questions that arose when
they stepped outside an identity defined by a profession and printed

on a business card or listed as bullet points on social media. Among themselves, they asked:

> We haven't said goodbye to titles, to what else? How do we do that?
> Do we need to have a label on ourselves?
> Is our career getting in the way of who we are?

In a focus group conversation addressing identity, the women of Cohort 25 raised more questions and spoke uneasily about not knowing how to introduce themselves after they retired. This university administrator described the difficulty she experienced when faced with a frequently posed question:

> I am getting used to the question 'What are you doing now?' I answer: 'Nothing.' Is that what I want ... *nothing*?

Many were very uncomfortable with the word "retired," but other adjectives seemed inadequate. Rather than referring to their former careers by saying "I was ..." some said they chose to identify themselves by describing what they were working on now: projects, books, philanthropy. Most soon realized that their titles and professional roles no longer fit the direction of their lives. Their career achievements, though significant and important in their development and identity, needed to be parsed and reexamined for the characteristics that once ensured success. Were those qualities and facets of their identity still important in retirement? How could they be flexed and adapted to their evolving lives?

Up until the point of their career transitions, the women of Cohort 25 usually had a plan. They were poised to look ahead and could envision the next steps and the new projects that would carry their careers forward. As they prepared to step outside their careers, the direction of the path ahead—even the path itself—was hard to discern. As they confronted this uncertain future, they were also confronting themselves. They were older, more experienced, and more certain about what they wanted and didn't want. They had developed a sense of who they were and what they needed. They were not the same people they had been when they started their careers in the mid-1960s and '70s. In fact, looking back, many of them might have agreed with the woman from Cohort 25 who said, "I had a career long before I had a sense of self."

Although not always referred to explicitly, "sense of self" was a concept that frequently came through in the comments from women of Cohort 25. When they reflected on their personal strengths and experiences as well as the origins of their values and their beliefs about self-worth and purpose, they were talking about the sense of self that had made them who they were. In the focus groups, they recognized what it took to develop and project a sense of self, and they expressed a strong desire to maintain it as they went forward.

The progression was extremely important, as the women in Cohort 25 moved from talking about titles, earned and awarded in the workplace, to reflecting on identity and a sense of self, personal and evolving over time. As women in the group queried one another and opened up about their experiences, they began to pose more personal questions: "What is the essence of who I am?" and "What do I have to offer?"

These were critical questions for many women. Just as their careers were highly individualized, so, too, the factors that shaped the codas to those careers were individual to each woman. What we heard among the women in the focus groups was mutual and unqualified encouragement to take the time needed and to think carefully about what the questions meant to each of them.

BRINGING IN THE WORD "POWER"

When members of one of the focus groups from Cohort 25 talked about the changes in identity they were anticipating after they left their careers, the conversation turned to the word "power." A successful entrepreneur put it this way: "People may say, 'I never defined myself by my career,' but we *had power* and enjoyed it."

Where did power come from in the careers of the women of Cohort 25? Sometimes, their power rested in the authority of being the owner, the person ultimately in charge of and responsible for a business or a professional practice. Or, a woman's power may have referred to a sense of agency, of being able to marshal and direct resources and the efforts of other people toward a common end. Individual women's career paths and opportunities offered many examples, but in general, the power of women from Cohort 25 lay in their ability *to make things happen*. Seen this way, women's power includes not only *authority* but also *agency*. Here are some of the ways women in Cohort 25 exercised power:)"

> *Making decisions* that shaped the direction of a business, university, or large institution: Individuals from Cohort 25 drove significant changes in the conceptual and physical design of cultural institutions, in the worldwide organization of scientific research. Sometimes, having power entailed

managing large budgets or creating or influencing policy, especially con-
cerning issues of equality and treatment of women.)"

Influencing and improving the lives of others: For some women, power originated in their ability to promote or help other people, whether through
building and leading a team; diagnosing and treating individuals with
physical or psychological problems; or providing life-changing personal
assessment and coaching. Another kind of power came in the form of
writing and implementing innovative curriculum that significantly
enriched children's educational experiences.)"

Having the freedom to imagine something new and finding a way to make it a
reality: Some women had access to resources that provided them with
the funding and staffs to not only be able to think creatively but also to
see their ideas become a reality. Power arose from using their imagina-
tion or ability for critical inquiry. Others worked independently, drawing
exclusively on their own talents and drive, starting and having the sole
control of a business, from the ground up.

The women of Cohort 25, like so many other Baby Boomers, were
told early on that they could do anything they set their minds to. The
force of those words emboldened them and became a driver throughout their careers. They believed they *could* do anything; they internalized that conviction and developed the confidence expected of them.
Although they took on complex and extremely challenging positions,
it was often without regard for recognition. They were driven to do
something *because they could*, because the opportunities were finally
available to women. Over the course of their careers, the women of
Cohort 25 exercised power within many levels of their respective
organizations, and although they might not have set out looking for
kudos, the power they acquired and exerted did bring them significant
recognition and rewards.

As women moved beyond their careers, how did the diminution of
power affect their sense of self? How did women who exercised
authority, who *could make things happen*, and who successfully took on
leadership, creative, and entrepreneurial responsibilities face the
"downsizing" of the scope of their power?

For some women, just talking about the role of power raised complex, personal issues. As one said, "Women always struggled with
the contrast of having power at work but not necessarily having it at
home." Because their professional lives were changing, perhaps coming to an end, women would no longer be in the position to exercise
the same power or agency as they had in their careers. However, the
experience they gained from understanding and wielding power on
many different levels would be a tremendous asset in settings beyond
the workplace.

How to be involved, what to offer, how to listen: these were all part of what it would take to find the best places and ways for women to invest their skills and experiences after leaving their careers. How did a person make the transition from having power in a professional setting to having an internalized sense of effectiveness and agency? How did one go from being in charge to being an effective and respected contributor? Perhaps women could call on a set of strategies that worked for them in the past: asking questions, listening, being quick studies. As we learned from their profiles, many women in this cohort took on professional positions for which they might not have been qualified—on paper, that is. They knew they could figure out what was needed and do it. That same flexibility and resourcefulness were very helpful again as women looked for opportunities to have an impact, to reach out and go after things.

STAYING VITAL AND FOCUSED: NOT THE SAME THING

In addition to bringing in concepts and language that gave new direction to the focus groups, the women in Cohort 25 also took exception to some of the assumptions we had brought to the groups. Most notable was our conflation of two distinct ideas into a single phrase. When we presented the following statement to the Cohort 25 focus groups for their consideration, we thought it was provocative and direct: "I'm concerned with staying vital and focused." And when the women in both focus groups identified it as being among their top three areas of interest, we were sure we had hit upon something of importance.

However, right away, and in both focus groups, held hundreds of miles from each other and a few months apart in time, the response was the same: staying *vital* and staying *focused* are very different things. What we had thought of as two ways of describing an essential quality of energy and clarity of purpose was quickly separated into two distinct qualities: being vital and being focused. And, the women made it clear: they are not the same thing!

In the conversations that followed, one woman's passion for her work and for her life came through loud and clear. She was proud of her successes and happy with the decision she made to sell her business when her husband was offered a professional position in another city that was too good to pass up. At the time the focus groups met, she was facing a dramatic, unexpected change in circumstances as her husband grappled with health problems. For her, the difference between being vital and being focused resonated in a very personal way:

> You can be energized and vital but absolutely lacking in focus, dashing from one thing to another without being able to settle down in a meaningful way. Or, you can be extremely focused but not feel vital; for example, the kind of focus demanded when caring for another person may be all-consuming and sap you of your own vitality.

As we listened to her, our preconceptions about the phrase we had drafted were thrown out. What we heard was not only instructive but also transformative, because the other women, too, challenged the assumptions it contained. Some women said achieving focus was easier after retirement because they had time to do more. Their children had finished college and become independent, and the demands and schedule of a full-time career were lifting. Others took a completely different view. They asserted that in order to be focused, it was important to have a job that was interesting, if not full-time. Some described how issues in women's lives, such as caregiving or family relationships, distracted them from concentrating on their own needs and passions, as did trepidation at the possibility of losing their mental or physical abilities.

AND THEN THERE IS PASSION

The conversations about vitality and focus moved easily to the subject of "passion," a word many women used when talking about their future. Pursuing a career, relocating, caring for others—all of these things can conspire to pull us away from what we might have once identified as our passion. As we leave our full-time careers, we have the opportunity to revisit and define again what we are passionate about. Some women in Cohort 25 were already doing this, returning to past interests, developing creative talents they had set aside. Some were testing out new ideas for putting their professional expertise to work in service of nonprofit or volunteer endeavors. For many, the first step was to reflect seriously on who they were and what they wanted to be doing after leaving their full-time careers.

After years of professional success in which women had proven themselves many times over, what exactly were their aspirations and dreams as they approached retirement? Sometimes serendipitous, sometimes calculated, the choices women made throughout their careers and lives assumed their own logic in hindsight. But how would they make decisions going forward? What would energize them? What were they looking for? What stood in the way?

The confidence, experience, and knowledge accrued during their careers were important resources as they moved forward. Women were not simply moving into retirement—they were *taking it on*. They were realizing just how much their abilities to balance multiple demands, take on new projects, and compose and lead successful teams had prepared them for life beyond the workplace. We learned about the concerns women were experiencing as they faced retirement, along with some of the obstacles they had encountered to doing things they wanted to do. Let's look more closely at what they were doing to confront and move past these concerns and obstacles and how they were assessing their personal situations and taking charge.

A NEW SENSE OF URGENCY, A DIFFERENT SENSE OF TIME

The women in Cohort 25 were taking charge in a new way. They often acknowledged that when they were young, they had no idea what they were up against. Their energy seemed limitless, as did the scope of what they could accomplish. As they moved into retirement, sustaining that energy was essential because there was so much they wanted to do. Knowing what they knew about themselves and the world, passion, too, had taken on a new importance. In the past, other priorities had sometimes prevented women from following and nurturing the things that were closest to their hearts. How would the wisdom and experience gained from a decades-long professional career empower them to return to those passions?

Just as they were facing the overarching questions of what to go after and how to prioritize, they were also facing small daily decisions about how to use their time. Even after several years of retirement, some women still exulted in being able to face each new, unstructured day. Others said they needed structure to feel productive. We have heard how some women guarded their time in retirement. The conundrum of seeing time as simultaneously infinite and finite jarred some women. Many referred to the vast open schedules that first made retirement feel like one long vacation, but then, their schedules began to fill as they accepted invitations to join new organizations and volunteer their time.

One woman described hoarding her time for research and for getting to the gym. As she put it, she had a sense of urgency for her project but not so much for the gym, so she found she needed to be very structured with her time. She said her sense of time had changed. She described it as a "big, floaty thing."

Women had begun to wonder how best to set boundaries, both within their families and in their communities. Getting involved with nonprofit boards or volunteering in an organization was attractive to many women, but they were quick to point out the pitfalls of overcommitting or thinking they could effect significant change. One woman was very explicit about the lessons she learned while being on what she called the "other side." In her former position, she saw people who had retired from prominent positions and who had come to her organization as volunteers, bringing what she described as the "I can make a difference here" mentality. "I don't want people to think I'm a jerk," she said. "People working in an organization have their jobs, and that needs to be recognized."

Regardless of whether they had retired, there was a strong consensus that women were not finished with what they considered important work. They still wanted to have an impact, to give the best of themselves, to share what they knew. They had come of age during a period when "developing a meaningful philosophy of life" was seen as a life goal by almost three-quarters of college freshmen.[1] How did that goal continue to drive the women as they moved into retirement?

The question came up several times. We asked women, and they asked one another: "What gives your life meaning?" Often the answer was "making an impact." The specifics for each woman varied: how she assessed her own ability to make an impact was highly personalized. Nonetheless, after years of building careers, pushing through barriers and breaking new ground, Baby Boomer women were still excited by the prospect of taking on challenges they could feel strongly about. Whether this meant turning lifelong commitments in a new direction or being energized by a sense of social responsibility, they were ready.

CURIOUS ABOUT OTHERS' EXPERIENCES

When we asked, "Why did you agree to be part of this project?" many women indicated a desire to engage with a group of their peers. They wanted to be able to share their own experiences and to hear about the experiences of others. They knew the essential qualities they shared with other women in the study—the same ten-year span of birth years and the decades spent as professionals—but they were curious about the rest of it: How did their experiences align with those of other women? What were others talking about and interested in as they approached the end of their full-time careers? Their comments suggested that this was something new for women who had not had the time or inclination to sit down and reflect with others about what they were experiencing in their lives or careers. We heard a consistent refrain in several women's responses. They were interested in *what they could learn* from talking with others: "I have not had the opportunity to think about these issues. I thought it would be uplifting and interesting sharing with others"; "I thought it would be interesting to be part of a study and meet other people who are smart . . . in my stage of life"; "I am looking to understand the process more and see what others are doing"; "I'm also interested in learning what others are doing/feeling at this stage of their lives"; "I feel like I am having to make a path again with few models. So I am interested in how others do it. Time is precious and limited and I want to make the most of what lies ahead"; and "I was very interested in being part of a discussion about this phase of life. I enjoy being part of a cohort that is strategizing about it and problem-solving."

Other women in Cohort 25 saw this research as an opportunity to look inward. They felt the study would be a way for them to engage in some valuable personal reflection. They wanted to connect the chapters of their personal stories—to look back in order to move ahead. The desire to find a bridge between the past and future was clearly heard in the comments of two women who had both been teachers and administrators. The first had spent her career in K–12 education, and the second had worked in higher education: "This is an opportunity to look back on my career and assess the strengths and weaknesses. It will allow me to discuss career choices and opportunities with others as I move forward in my life" and "It sounded interesting and might help me gain some insight into how to make this next phase more satisfying."

The twin desires—to learn from others and to engage in self-reflection—were motivations we encountered many times. These Baby Boomer women—who had had long, successful careers—were, as a group, ready to think and talk about their experiences. They not only had a breadth of insight and much to share, but they also wanted to know more about themselves. As a group, the women of Cohort 25 were very self-aware and thoughtful. They wanted to make good decisions for themselves as well as with and on behalf of others they cared about. They might not have had much formal guidance counseling forty or fifty years earlier, but the years they spent pursuing careers and balancing professional and private lives had taught them invaluable lessons about who they were as they approached retirement. As they moved into the next phase, they recognized the importance of paying attention to their own interests, playing to their strengths, and finding ways to follow their passion.

BECOMING THEIR OWN ROLE MODELS

Early in the interviewing process, we often heard women say they had no role models for making the transition beyond their full-time career. Taking this as a cue, we formulated this statement for the focus groups to consider: "Lack of a role model is a hindrance to my next steps."

The response was overwhelming: "We don't need role models!" What had emerged in the interviews as an observation was apparently just that, an observation about the lack of role models, but *not* a call for help. The focus group participants were emphatic in saying that just as they had made their own way in their careers with few, if any, women to follow, now that they were making a transition to something new, they were confident in their abilities to find their own way, perhaps individually, perhaps as a group. This confidence in their ability to "figure it out" echoed the conviction with which they had made earlier career moves without always knowing what lay ahead.

Rather than looking for models in the generations that came before them, they were, instead, recognizing the uniqueness of their professional lives and turning to themselves and their peers for ideas and advice about moving forward. If anything, women in this group were each other's role models; they were looking for ways to encourage, cheer each other on, and share their concerns and fears. The women in one focus group said it plainly: "We are the matriarchs now." Energetic and creative, they were nonetheless grandmothers and great-aunts. In some families, they were indeed the oldest generation, putting a new face on the concept of "matriarch." What did that label suggest to them and to their families? How were they going to embody and pass on the values of a generation?

Although women recognized the value in becoming role models for one another, they were also keenly aware of what they had to offer others. "We need to find a new place for our wisdom to be used." As a group, these women had always believed that earlier generations' expectations for women did not apply to them, but at this point in their lives, they were mindful of the example they were setting for the next generation. They believed that the decisions they made and how they remained actively engaged after their full-time careers had the potential to influence younger career women. One woman said it clearly, "How we enter this phase will provide valuable information to the next generation."

Talking with one another, women expressed deep concerns about the demands and sacrifices faced by young professional women. Their comments were blunt, sometimes unsettling. One woman's comments were grounded in both empathy and concern: "Something seems to have gone wrong with women who are working now. ... They have been schnookered into doing everything ... young women who are working, having babies, etc. They will be fried by forty. What are they thinking?"

Another woman, who for years balanced her design career with raising a family and finding time for volunteering, worried that the demands being placed on young women would make it impossible for them to give back to their communities in the ways that were needed to support the arts and cultural institutions: "What are the implications for communities, arts institutions, etc. when the generation that follows us doesn't have the time to serve as volunteer teachers, fundraisers, and docents?"

Whether as role models or mentors, mothers or grandmothers, women were realizing that decisions they made would come to represent the values and legacy of their generation of professional women. For years, they broke barriers, opened doors, and balanced family and professional obligations to change the expectations and opportunities available to girls and women. As they approached the end of their careers, they had the opportunity to frame another set of expectations. What was the next phase? What could professional women look forward to after they left their full-time careers? What shared factors affected their decisions?

Just about everyone in Cohort 25 mentioned factors that could be considered external: concerns about relationships, housing, finances, and health care. But there were also powerful internal factors, psychological and emotional elements of women's lives. In focus group conversations, women talked about the importance of recognizing and dealing with these internal factors. To sort out competing responsibilities, women said they must understand and acknowledge their own needs, and when it came to looking ahead, they needed to be realistic.

WANTING TO WORK, BEING REALISTIC

Nowhere is the need to be realistic more critical than in women's plans for working, whether full- or part-time, as they get older. As one consultant said, "Nobody gets to be our age who doesn't feel lucky to be able to work." Finding work would require very different strategies than were needed to enter the workplace thirty or more years earlier. Even though some professions, especially those where one worked remotely or online, might be welcoming to older workers, the coaching and recruiting professionals in Cohort 25 spoke candidly about the difficulties faced by people looking for work in their fifties and sixties. If a woman's objective was to continue working, how could she assess how realistic her goals were when some organizations and firms would not consider applicants over sixty years of age?

If a woman wanted to work less than full-time, looking for a position that offered satisfaction, and perhaps some income, meant being realistic about several factors. It might mean actively networking and looking for an opportunity if she wanted to change direction or explore something new. Beyond connections and luck, finding a job might require resilience and new skills. At this point in their working lives, most women had a strong sense of the kind of work they wanted to do and of how much time they wanted to commit to working after retirement. These factors, too, played a role.

Going after a second career or dream job, even a part-time one, could be tough. Sometimes, the realities of the workplace made it difficult, if not impossible, to move in a new direction. After leaving a demanding, high-profile career with an international agency, one woman was hoping to enter an entirely different work setting. Following her passion for art, she took flower-arranging classes and approached several florist shops, looking for part-time employment. As much as she wanted to reinvent her working life, she was repeatedly turned down. Her lack of experience was seen as a barrier, even when she offered to work for free. Although everything seemed possible when this cohort of women first entered the workplace, as they neared or entered retirement, the realities of a changed economy, combined with perceptions about older workers, created a work environment in which opportunities were much more limited.

FEELING COMPETENT, STAYING CONNECTED

One of the focus groups made an insightful connection *between* these concerns, saying they worried that they could lose touch and lose competency *because of* changes in technology. When they considered how much they relied on technology, along with the constant changes it brought, they realized it would not take long for a small change to have a large impact. A person leaving a career in which emerging technologies, new devices, and constant updates were part of the workplace could easily feel vulnerable to falling behind once she left that environment. New developments in technology could not only make it difficult for women to move back into the workforce, even part-time, but also prevent them from feeling they were still competent and savvy.

CLEARING A SPACE

Women in both focus groups talked about preparing for the psychological aspects of retirement. After years of working in structured, goal- and project-driven careers, women were now facing a period of their lives where structure and rewards were less clear. "Our goals may need to be smaller," one woman observed. When unforeseeable factors made it seem as though things were beyond one's control, or when health concerns—her own or those of her loved ones—became a major problem, the challenge to maintain an independent, vibrant life could be enormous. Setting goals might seem much less important than the engaged *process* of living one's life, but even that could be complicated. One woman asked directly, "How do I keep living my own life, without feeling guilty?"

As women prepared themselves psychologically and emotionally for the changes that would accompany the transition beyond their careers, some mentioned the need to clear things away or pause for a time. One woman said she was very conscious that "if you let it evolve, something will happen." Another knew she "[would] always be doing something." As she put it, "I have cleared a path." For a woman who spent a long career in the academic world, her self-confidence and resourcefulness were keys to preparing for what might come next. She realized, "I want to leverage my wisdom rather than learn new skills."

FACING THE REALITIES OF AGING

The physical realities of aging were irrefutable. Talking together in focus groups, women emphasized that they were not afraid of getting old, even though they were well aware of the realities of being the oldest person in an office or having trouble renting a car at age seventy. They *were* afraid of being seen as "old ladies." Conversations on this subject covered everything from facing ageism to considering a face-lift. The same women who, looking back, realized that gender bias was often part of their work environment now freely acknowledged the pervasiveness of prejudice based on age. Beyond the external anti-dotes offered by cosmetic surgery, salon treatments, and spandex, how should women respond to the demeaning remarks and attitudes of ageism? How should accomplished, professional women deal with others' perceptions without being further dismissed as being defensive or shrill? This retired businesswoman posed an unequivocal question: "We spent our careers being trivialized as women. Are we going to be doubly trivialized as old women?"

For the women of a generation whose demographic shorthand, "Baby Boomer," often connoted energy and stylish vigor, growing older meant seeing themselves, as well their friends and their generation of authors, actors, athletes, and politicians, changing in appearance and, eventually, in physical well-being and stamina. How women looked as they aged and how they thought they should look were often based on stereotypes of active, young-looking older people. The loss of a youthful appearance at the same time one was losing her professional identity was especially troubling. As if they were literally being erased from others' view, many women described how easily one became invisible in a culture that placed high value on physical appearance and youth. The potential loss of experience, talent, and knowledge that accompanied that erasure could be enormous. However, as we will see, many women from Cohort 25 were drawing on their personal and professional experiences in ways that asserted their presence and their desire to remain engaged. They were determined to remain *visible*.

NOTE

1. Jean M. Twenge, Elise C. Freeman, and W. Keith Campbell, "Generational Differences in Young Adults' Life Goals, Concern for Others, and Civic Orientation, 1966–2009," *Journal of Personality and Social Psychology* 102, no. 5 (2012): 1049.

6

"What's New?"

A year or so after we conducted the first interviews and focus groups, we contacted the women of Cohort 25 again and invited them to participate in a follow-up phone call. We wondered if having the year to reflect on their experiences would have changed their feelings about retirement. We were also curious about what they had taken away from the focus group conversations. Did the responses and camaraderie generated by the focus groups affect them as they moved through their transition to retirement? All twenty-five women responded immediately to our invitation. Twenty-three of them were able to speak with us by telephone, and we communicated with the last two through exchanges of e-mail. We purposely kept our questions informal and open-ended. We asked, "What's going on?" and "What insights, if any, have you had since we last talked?"

After having had time to think about the transitional process they were going through, the women were open, enthusiastic, and optimistic. Some of the concerns they had expressed in the interviews came up again, especially increasing or changing family responsibilities and the sudden realization for some that they had become the oldest women in their families. Other worries, especially about aging and loss, were still there but were expressed differently. Women acknowledged the inevitability of loss, but rather than being anxious about it, they used it as the impetus to focus on and enjoy their lives in the present. Most surprising was the large number and the consistency of *new* things the women talked about: the value of friendship, the importance of remaking their physical space, and most importantly, the changes in identity that had invigorated them.

They felt comfortable returning to elements of their past; sometimes, this included facing painful memories and, in other cases, interests or talents they had set aside. Simultaneously, they were looking ahead to their future with a new sense of purpose. The women talked openly about finding a new identity and having a new understanding of what being retired meant to them. And they were happy.

HOW DID IT HAPPEN?

What allowed the women of Cohort 25 to move past their feelings of uncertainty and fear to reach a new stage of contentment and self-confidence? Throughout this project, they had examined their professional lives from many angles. The effect of the multistep research process was to allow them to tell the stories of their careers in different ways many times and then to begin to edit those stories, adding details and refocusing them, as they made new discoveries about themselves. As they completed the survey, they were able to look back at the broad sweep of their professional lives, from girlhood to retirement.

During the interviews, the focus of the women was inward as they recalled their personal successes and the challenges they encountered. In the focus groups, they stepped outside their own stories and connected to others, brainstorming and gathering ideas they could endorse as a group. It is important to remember that the focus group format—in which the women could speak freely, set the direction, and develop their own answers—encouraged the participants to keep thinking and talking about their career transition after the group sessions were over.

When we reached out to them a year later, they had had time for individual reflection, not directed by us but set in motion by the questions they had raised and answered for themselves. Many of the women spoke enthusiastically about changes in their lives. Many of their fears had been eased by speaking candidly about the "elephants in the room." Whether death or illness, loss of a sense of identity, or the possibility of being absorbed by the caregiving needs of others, the things that worried them had come out in the open. After discovering that they shared more than career and workplace experiences with one another, the women in Cohort 25 realized they were part of a compassionate, formidable, and articulate group of peers. They shared many of the same fears, but those fears were mitigated by the process of talking about them with others.

Many of the women were still working, and many had continuing caregiving responsibilities, but they were also focusing on *new* concerns: their spouse's retirement, the desire for a satisfying network of friends, and the efforts required to remake or find a physical location to meet their personal and professional needs. Women were looking closely at the essential elements of who they were and choosing to connect to their historical and emotional roots. They were finding new ways to explore talents and interests they had set aside and were using the skills and expertise from their career for new purposes. They were making decisions about what they needed and how to find it. For most, a deliberate process of self-reflection and talking with others had brought them to a new and satisfying acceptance of themselves.

"I Think My Spirit Is Coming Back"

In general, the women talked about how their thoughts on retirement had evolved through a process of discarding. Some had spoken about their fears of slipping into the role of housewife or losing their identity after they left their career, but once they were able to talk about these things and discover they were not alone, they realized their fears were unfounded. What they did next, and very successfully, was redraft a new image of themselves in retirement. As one woman described it, "I had to look for a new profile, to define myself with a new profile. What looked like disparate pieces with no cohesion suddenly came together."

Women who were still working continued to talk to others who had already retired; doing so took away some of the fear of the unknown about what life would be like after their career. They spoke of a period of introspection, private and perhaps unexpected, in which their thoughts about life after retirement took on a new clarity. They were able to let go of fears and acknowledge their individual strengths, responsibilities, and curiosities with a new sense of acceptance. They were facing the question of *what's next* in a very positive way. The enthusiasm and optimism we heard repeatedly were reflected in the comments of these three women: "Mature acceptance. I don't have the physical stamina—so what?"; "The conversation I had with you got me thinking about what things meant to me and what I needed to do . . ."; and "Your project made me realize how much women supporting women *supports* women—I had forgotten how powerful that is."

Shifting from the high energy demands of a career to another phase was a dramatic change, but women were drawing on their strengths of flexibility and adaptability to move forward, just as they had throughout their careers. The same strengths that made them good listeners, supportive colleagues, and respected leaders were again empowering them to help one another. This peer-to-peer support among women was vital as they sorted out and modeled the identities and behaviors that were changing how they and others viewed retirement. Perhaps most importantly, when they spoke to us, they were still figuring things out.

"I Want to Keep the Creative Part, Not the Drudgery"

Work was still part of their lives, but the women saw it differently now. Forty percent of them were still working full-time when we followed up with them. Sixty percent had transferred their work-based skills and expertise into part-time work or extensive volunteer activities. Many of those who had left full-time careers still loved working, in some capacity, but what excited them most were creative, problem-solving projects in which they worked closely with others and brought together the skills, strategies, and contacts that they had developed in their career. Whether full-time or part-time, the women described being choosy about how and where they worked as we heard in the words of these two women: "I am 65, so it's interesting because business has taken off in the last three years. I am being more selective, and plan to retire at 70, unless I have an illness or something . . . but not with the same hours or extremely consuming schedule; I would like to work four days a week and be more flexible" and "I am doing lots of part-time small business consulting, where I can step in and step out without being brought into the day-to-day; I want to keep the creative part going, not the drudgery."

There were also things the women missed about working. No one mentioned the loss of an office or support staff, but what they did miss was the sense of agency that accompanied their careers. Without accountability, structure, or authority, they no longer had the same ability to move projects forward. A retired university administrator described it this way: "I was a little naive in any idea I had about how to mobilize things without authority." And another woman spoke candidly about the challenges of working independently, without an externally imposed structure: "I am still working on a project, with great enthusiasm and approaching some tangible outcomes, but with no external deadlines or accountability, you can keep going down a rabbit hole, without producing something useful."

"Looking at My Friends, I Know Retirement Is Possible"

Women who were still working full-time were also looking around. They were watching and talking to friends who had retired, checking to see how and what they were doing. At the time of our follow-up telephone conversation, one woman was planning to make a decision about her retirement in the upcoming months. All but one of her closest friends at the university where she worked had retired, so she knew it was possible. "That makes it a little easier," she said. Knowing that friends were flourishing and that they had made decisions and moved to a new phase of their lives was very reassuring for those still in the workplace.

Some people certainly had an easier time than others. Did the type of work a woman performed affect the difficulty of her transition? One woman thought so. Although she was still working full-time, she had made her own correlation between the nature of a woman's work and her response to retirement:

> There is something about people hitting retirement: Some want to work forever, some are thrilled not to be working. The women whose work lives have been structured can't decide what to do with the lack of structure. "What do I do with all this time?"

She gave the example of a friend who was a judge and who "nearly had a nervous breakdown when she retired," but other friends who worked for themselves and had more freedom in how they organized their days seemed to make the transition more easily. She described their ability to adapt with these words: "They were used to having lives where they did multitasking."

Another woman who was consciously spending more time away from work in anticipation of her retirement found that the new schedule was having quite an effect on her. When we asked, "What are you discovering when you take time away?" she answered, "I am less content and more emotional." The sense of being unsettled during the transition to retirement affected each woman differently and, as we discovered, lasted much longer for some than for others.

"I Talk to My Parents Every Day"

For many women, their elderly parents or relatives continued to be a great concern and responsibility. Others also had the responsibility of caring for spouses, children, and grandchildren. As we saw earlier, women were worried about how they would continue to maintain their own identities and interests when they faced caregiving needs in retirement. In fact, a year after their interviews, we learned that the women were successfully managing those responsibilities. Whether by building the needs of others into their daily routine, staying in touch by phone with parents who lived far away, or putting a trusted caregiving team in place, women were figuring out how to devise a plan that worked for them and their loved ones. One woman chose to use the word "caretaking" and compared it to another familiar role: "Caretaking is like being a mother. It does not define me or hold me back; it just reshapes my day and energy. Caretaking must be done with compassion. Then everything changes."

Two other women from Cohort 25, both still working, were very aware of the growing needs of their parents: "My parents are older and I am always thinking about whether I need to be there to take care of them. I talk to them every day" and "Our parents need more help, but our lives haven't changed. We are still doing what we have always done ... There's no magic answer to 'what's the next step?' I turned seventy this year. I am still working, and my ego, or something, says 'keep going.' "

For a woman who lived abroad, far from her relatives in America, caregiving brought a special sense of responsibility: "The biggest change for me is the increased *feeling* of responsibility for elderly relatives, both arranging for a team of caregivers and taking on legal responsibilities."

"How Did That Happen So Fast?"

Several women in the cohort talked about the shift in perspective and identity that took place within their family after they had made decisions on behalf of infirm parents or experienced the death of their parents. One acknowledged, "For me, it was acceptance of the role as older woman within the family. I wasn't anticipating that."

Another woman recognized how much she had been affected by sudden changes in her mother's health:

> The biggest shift is becoming a parent to my mom. At first it fell solely to me to be caretaker. My mother had been living on her own, but within a few weeks, her health suddenly deteriorated. I didn't realize how much pressure and responsibility I was under ... it was an eye-opener.

A third woman spoke poignantly about how her mother's death changed the generational relationships in their family: "The most disconcerting thought—I am now the older generation. How did that happen so fast? With one less person to be worried about [her mother was constantly on her mind and had died in the past year], your whole perspective shifts."

The change in identity the women described, after a parent entered a nursing home or died, may evoke memories from other periods of change, for example, when their children grew up and left home. As they accepted and adjusted to the loss and the changes it brought, they discovered they had arrived at a very different place in their lives; they had fewer responsibilities, more free time, and increased opportunities to pursue their own interests.

"I Hope It's Not My Job to Entertain Him"

For women who were married or in committed relationships, making plans about the future was not done in isolation. Their retirement transition often coincided with the retirement of their spouse or partner, and together, they were figuring out what that meant for the years ahead. Several women talked about the impact of their spouse's impending retirement. For one woman, her husband's retirement meant stopping and then starting again:

> I found my rhythm, but dealing with my retirement was also dealing with my husband's retirement until he accepted a new full-time job. He was asked to come back, so it's not the same as if it were just another new job. We were on the brink of a new phase and now have to be flexible in putting the pieces together again. Once you think you've got it, it changes again. That's this stage of life.

And another woman, who continued to work on a major research project in her retirement, wondered what retirement from a professional career would mean for her husband:

> My husband is retiring soon. The intersections of our lives will change; negotiating what that will mean. What is the point of retirement? I have been able to keep my professional interests and my involvement with community organizations, but he cannot do his professional work outside a professional setting. My retirement is a continuum of myself and work; his will be a much more dramatic shift.

A third woman, whose husband had also not yet retired, was concerned about his finding satisfying groups or activities in which to be engaged: "I hope it's not my job to entertain him. I guess basically I am fairly selfish. He is on boards, has founded a company, but I wonder if he will find things he likes, perhaps book clubs or research, as satisfying as I do."

At least one woman had reevaluated the importance of a personal relationship as other things in her life were changing: "I am less and less dependent, more indifferent to the man I have been seeing."

Although fundamental commitments shaped women's lives and affected their decisions going forward, new elements came into play as well. Aspects of their lives they might have taken for granted or put off to the side were now assuming a new importance. Most valued among these were friends.

RECONNECTING, REACHING OUT, GOLFING, AND LISTENING

Many women talked about the importance of reaching out to old friends and actively pursuing new friendships. For those who were single, dealing with the loss of a ready social network of coworkers was especially difficult, and making friends outside the workplace could be a brand-new experience. More than one woman used language associated with dating and marriage to refer to the challenge of meeting new friends.

This woman described the difficulty of meeting people:

> Now I don't have the responsibility of stopping in, taking her out [her mother has recently moved into an assisted living facility]; I have big time/spaces in my life, therefore, I am also re-creating a social life for myself. It's not easy to find new friends as a mid-sixties divorced woman . . . my experience of making friends in the past was always in the context of school or work. Now, without that context, the challenge is how to re-create something other than what was there before. It's like someone who has lost a spouse. I realized that this is something I need to put a *conscious effort* into.

Another woman found golf to be a natural way to connect with others: "I have expanded my social circle. It's a magic thing on a golf course. If you want to be paired up, it's like speed dating, getting into a community through informal, coincidental meetings."

Whether it was reaching out to old friends or taking time to meet with and listen to others, there was a deliberateness and emphasis on the importance of the action itself. After several moves and a return to the area where she had grown up, this woman was reconnecting: "I am contacting friends I haven't had time to be with. This is a *big* priority."

One woman who hadn't yet retired was testing what it would be like to get to know others beyond her professional world: "I have also been seeking out different people to talk to outside my business/professional network and experimenting more . . . Maybe it's part of the story—taking more time away from work to see what that *feels like* . . . I am listening to things differently."

MAKING A NEW PLACE FOR THEMSELVES: WHERE TO LIVE, WHERE TO WORK

Another area in which women were deliberately focusing their energy was choosing and shaping a physical environment for themselves. This may have meant buying or building or remodeling a home, as this woman did: "I purchased a house at the shore and am now in the middle of renovations."

Or it may have meant carving out space where they could work, especially if they had downsized and were sharing limited space. For this artist, making a new physical space involved redesigning her work environment after selling her business: "My studio space is transformed! I'm really happy; it's better than I anticipated!"

Women were changing their physical space to make it an attractive, comfortable, and suitable setting for work and other interests. Two people described how finding the right workspace required flexibility and resourcefulness: "I have taken care of the logistics. I have a place outside my home to write: the library" and "I'm thinking about where to put a desk for him and one for me after my husband's retirement."

Some women had moved to new cities or were anticipating a dramatic move to resettle themselves for the future. As one woman explained, "I am looking for a base outside France." Whether it was setting up a new base or moving to be near friends or family, the move to a new city could bring both cultural and personal adjustments. Moving to a smaller city raised serious questions for one woman:

> The biggest thing I have learned is that where I chose to retire (a small city in Pennsylvania) is very different from where I lived before, so I ask myself, *Where can I add value here? Where do I want to put my energy?* I don't regret the move at all, but I do see it as an "unnatural habitat," compared to New York City or Philadelphia.

Sometimes, the flexibility offered by retirement produced a kind of rootlessness, as we heard from another woman. She was still working but was able to do so at a distance while her husband pursued other interests. When we spoke by phone, she and her husband were spending the winter in California, where he was playing golf:

> The sense of being "off to my next home" always keeps me from settling in as much as I want. I am always looking for the next rental. . . . I don't want to make a long-term commitment because of the constant moving.

DRAWING ON "WHO I AM" TO MOVE FORWARD

As they began to take charge of their time and create a space where they could feel settled and productive, many women were looking for ways to return to interests and experiences that were important to them in the past. This may have involved reconnecting to a personal experience that was fundamental to a woman's past and identity or developing a talent she had set aside to concentrate on her career. Or perhaps, it meant finding a way to put the knowledge from her career to a new use. In any case, many women described their experiences of going back and drawing on an earlier part of themselves as deeply satisfying and emotionally powerful.[1] Two women returned to elements of their lives that had shaped their experiences from childhood. The first found a way to draw on her experiences as a child in order to help immigrant families:

> I did in fact take on a new project—somewhat time-consuming but very exciting. I have organized a discussion group for immigrants and their families. I have gone full circle. It reminded of my own experience of being embarrassed by my parents' accents and then being ashamed of that feeling ... My professional work had stimulated childhood memories of when I was the child of immigrants. I was alone with it, and my mother was alone with it. The first event I organized had people from eighteen different countries, all eager to talk.

Another woman returned to Bergen-Belsen, the Nazi concentration camp and later displaced persons camp where she was born. This experience affected her profoundly and brought a new focus to her work:

> I went back to see the place where my parents met and married and where I was born. It was an incredible experience for me. It made me think that in the next chapter or continuing chapter of my life I'd like to do something in Holocaust studies. The trip to Bergen-Belsen was a catharsis of sorts, but not closure. I want to impact people who may not even know about the past. I want to educate people about what happens when you hate, when you see differences more than similarities.

Both of these women described the life-altering transformation that took place when they were able to return to painful events that shaped their families and their own lives. They were effectively adding brand-new chapters to the stories of who they were and where they had come from. As adults approaching the traditional age of retirement, they had found ways to connect with and create something positive from the suffering of their parents. For both women, these new, positive experiences took place within the months following their interviews. Each of them had made a dramatic commitment that took her work and life in a new direction.

Not all of the women in Cohort 25 experienced such profound epiphanies. Yet, many did talk about another kind of joy—that of finding time for passions they had once set aside. When women spoke of embracing their talents or interests, their voices rose with excitement. A woman whose musical talent was first recognized in childhood said, "I am happily involved in a women's singing group. Their mission is bringing joy to others." After a successful career in health care, another woman found joy in returning to her interest in visual art: "I did art in college, and hadn't gotten back to it, but I love getting back to oil painting now."

Some of the women in Cohort 25 were just starting to think about returning to an earlier passion. They were still trying to figure out what would be involved and how they might reconnect. In our follow-up phone call, one woman told us she was thinking of embarking on an entirely new area of academic study:

> Despite my law background, I think I would like to be an engineer ... There were *zero* women in engineering when we were undergrads ... We hear about reconnecting with what we were as kids; I had that mechanical/mathematic ability as a kid, but I never developed it.

And another woman discovered that returning to the creative interests she had set aside could have collateral benefits:

> I have come to realize some of my creative talents (which I had lost time for during my business career) are still of major interest to me. For me that means various crafts that will bring me a small "pocket change" income and lead me to new relationships. I am still not settled on how to capitalize on marketing this talent, but that is the next step I am focused on.

Another way of drawing on "who I am" to move forward is to find a way to make use of professional skills outside the workplace. The woman who described rediscovering the potential in her creative talents also candidly assessed the expertise she had that could help others. Then she found a meaningful way to put that expertise to use:

> It is clear that when you leave your career, the things that drew you towards that career are still very much a part of your core, but in a different way. I am no longer striving to "climb that career ladder" but eager to give back some of my expertise. For instance, operations and logistics were very much a large part of my career. I have made a decision to run for a board position in my homeowners' association. I feel that I could make a significant contribution to organizing logistics and operations while at the same time satisfying a part of me.

ACCEPTING THEMSELVES

When we asked women what insights they had had in the months following their interviews, they identified one important quality in common: they were paying close attention to and accepting what they had learned about themselves.

With a confirmed sense of her own vitality, this businesswoman, working part-time and only on projects she purposefully chose, recognized that she was defying some people's stereotypes of older women:

> I feel I'm as vital now as I was when I was 30 . . . We're marginalized, in a cutesy grandmother role. Hell, no! You didn't define me then; you're not going to define me now.

For another woman, discoveries about herself were the product of years of experience:

> I have come to the realization that being a "member" of anything is not going to work for me. Having been a leader in a corporate environment will not allow me to stop being a leader. The hardest part of adjusting to retirement will be to somehow integrate my leadership skills into whatever path I pursue while trying not to allow this pursuit to overcome my newly found freedom.

Others who were still working had also learned important things about themselves. One woman had happily discovered that as things had stabilized within the new leadership of her organization, other people were beginning to appreciate her more. This, in turn, had encouraged her to reveal more of her personality and to trust in the respect and friendship of those around her. She described the change this way:

> At work, I can do more of what I want to do. It has taken three years, because things were all up in the air all the time. It's now eighty percent stable, and employees are starting to come to me, realizing I'm a real person and fun.

The urgency of always being available and committed to work had diminished for a second woman—also still working—who recognized and accepted a shift in herself: "I always thought I had to respond immediately [to keep/develop business], but it now feels okay to say, 'I can't do that for a week.' "

For another woman, self-acceptance meant understanding what would keep her motivated. She described how she had become more focused and deliberate in seeking out support for her work: "There's every reason in the world not to write, so I went to a meeting of authors and picked out some people to form an authors' group. We meet once a month and that means I have a deadline, even though I don't yet have a publisher."

This same woman, stirred by her husband's retiring, also realized it was important to her to be more selective in her volunteer commitments: "I have a huge appetite for getting involved, but I have had to exercise prudence and discipline. For example, I am shedding board commitments that don't connect to something important in my life."

Whether by paring down their outside commitments or thinking about work in a new way, women were making decisions for themselves, based on what they had learned. They were asking themselves, "What makes me happy? What makes me feel connected and productive?" One woman enthusiastically described her high level of activity:

> I would not be happy sitting and playing mahjong. I need so much more intellectual stimulation. I am running at capacity. Not ready to stop that. My days are full and that means a great deal to me. I feel good, and I think often there is so much I still want to accomplish. I want to live a long time, I hope my eyesight remains strong and I can maintain the kind of independence that will allow me to do so.

As women experimented with finding the right balance, their efforts were occasionally at odds with the desire to help others. This former higher education administrator learned that her "usual M.O. of throwing myself in 150%" could create problems. Sometimes she felt she was sacrificing part of her own interest in support of other people. She said she was still figuring out why she did that. She reflected further:

> Sometimes I feel like my own interests and time are taking a back seat. Recentering [a word she first used in her interview] is still a struggle. On a daily basis, in my life, I have interests that get disrupted.

Another woman, still heavily involved in her career, wanted to ensure that the balance of work and leisure she envisioned would remain intact: "I was determined to make sure it stayed true. It took some effort, adjusting to the fact that it is okay at my age to protect my time and enjoy life."

The desire to protect their time and the fear of overcommitment encouraged many women to carefully marshal their time and energy, as one woman stated, "I'm busy, but not overcommitted; that was my

goal." For another woman, finding the right balance required impos-
ing and staying on a schedule:

> I need to balance how to continue community commitments and meet
> goals for myself. I still have a very structured week and calendar. I keep
> my time structured and predictable and continue getting my work done
> and getting time at the gym.

Time is not only a valued, finite quality, but it is also the medium
that is required for thoughtful reflection and introspection to flourish.
Women in Cohort 25 often talked about needing time to think and sort
things out. Many described how important it was to allow some time
to pass in order to reflect and explore what they really wanted to do
after they left their full-time careers. This woman's experience provided a good example:

> In retrospect, during my first year of retirement I was, shall I say, head-
> ing in a lot of different directions as to what my next steps would be. It
> is almost as if I was scattered in what my interests were and feeling pres-
> sured in establishing a time line, trying to piece together "what is next."
> I learned in this past year that I needed to slow down and explore. I have
> done that through interacting with people in my new community but all
> the while not making any real commitments until I was totally sure that
> there was a clear direction—a direction that will provide a sense of lead-
> ership and accomplishment.

For another woman, it took much longer to free her schedule and
settle into doing what she enjoyed: "This is the first year I have felt like
I don't have a schedule ... my 'going to the office days' ended seven
years ago, and it has taken this long to have an open schedule. We
asked, "What helped that?" and her answer addressed both the pas-
sage of time and the introspection she experienced through writing
and reading: "I have given myself permission to write more and to
quit reading a book if I don't like it."

On the other hand, when we spoke to another woman, who was
hoping to work to age seventy, she had turned away from the idea
she once had for writing a book. As she put it, she realized she doesn't
need to *do* certain things:

> It's hard to be significant in life; you have to be realistic about the impact
> you can make as an individual ... Probably the best contribution you
> can make is to be a good person, and what's most important is raising
> children, being a good citizen of the world, being a good American,
> not being too selfish, enjoying family and helping them.

She was not alone in thinking about what it means to make a difference. Is having an impact beyond one's own life and family even possible? In talking about the insights they had had in the year since their interviews, several women from Cohort 25 were careful to define what making a difference meant for them at that point in their lives:

> I'm open to things, but it has to appeal to me spiritually, not in a religious sense, but feed my spirit creatively, feed me or give me a sense of making a positive difference in a way that appeals to me ... I'm not a do-gooder.

Another woman who had been working full-time when we first met had retired and settled into a very different life a year later. She was physically active, teaching a little, and "enjoying it just as it is. I'm not stressed about making a contribution to the world." After a career spent in a demanding academic and research environment, she said, "When I want to make a difference, I write a check, and that feels fine." Others easily described insights they had about their own sense of contentment. Two women made the point that the changes that came with retirement did not feel like a loss. In answer to the question "What insights have you had since we last talked?" one answered, "My insights? I am surprised by how contented I am. I always had eight hundred balls in the air, but now I have three to four." And the other said, "My insights? I have been living the dream: retired, enjoying it, but I don't feel there's a huge hole in my world. I am teaching one course, both online and on campus, per year, as it fits my schedule."

What do the women's insights tell us? As much as they continued to challenge themselves with new projects and new commitments, the women were also embracing a frank self-awareness. A year after the interviews and focus groups, they were no longer worried about a loss of identity or the possibility of becoming irrelevant when they stopped working. Instead, they were taking charge of new identities and being very selective about where they put their energy. They were also realistic about the inevitability of loss, often seeing it as a motivator. As one woman put it, "It's a nice time of life, but scary because things are so good." Others echoed this sentiment. One woman had been influenced by a recent experience: "What has increased is my desire to do things while I have the ability, a lesson from my post-surgery time." Another described coming to a realization that changed her outlook: "One thing that's different for me in the last year is this realization: 'It's a wake-up call, life is a finite experience and there is an endgame.'"

What Are You Doing Now?

When we asked the women of Cohort 25 this question, their responses were charged with confidence and excitement. They had sharpened their thinking and invested time in learning about volunteer opportunities that interested them. Some were redirecting their professional expertise, teaching part-time in a field where they were uniquely qualified or reaching out to others to offer professional help or guidance.

We were most impressed by the number of *new* activities the women of Cohort 25 had taken on in the year following their interviews: one woman had become involved in an effort to get people of color on boards of major corporations; another was working with widows of the 9/11 tragedy; and a third had become an active member of the national alumni leadership council for her college, where she enjoyed being able to make a difference in the life of students: "And I feel appreciated here."

In several cases, women had expanded their involvement in areas they felt strongly about: One woman had taken on new leadership responsibilities for the council board of an international museum, something she had not had time to do before. Another's commitment to her writing had gained a new focus when a memoir-writing course she took evolved into a monthly writing group. Others had gone from having an idea to getting involved: joining a homeowners board, learning more about animal shelters. A woman who had begun to act on her interest in animal shelter work through training and volunteering summed up this new level of commitment: "More actions than just thinking about it."

In their responses to the question about what they were doing, the women of Cohort 25 consistently conveyed their excitement about the future, as one woman asserted, "I just turned sixty-five, and I am definitely trying to make this the beginning of a new phase, and to grab opportunities." Two other women specifically mentioned discoveries they had made that had helped them understand themselves differently. After a long corporate career, one said, "[I realized] that when you leave your career the things that drew you towards your career are still very much a part of your core, but in a different way." Another described her insight this way: "I realized the absolute importance of shaking things up in order to feel alive again, to take that risk and walk into a place where you don't know what it will feel like. I am not sure exactly what's going to happen, but working in the studio and working on expansion of consciousness is there for me, a new focus."

The women of Cohort 25 were making it clear; they were not settling down to quiet lives in retirement.

WITH ACCEPTANCE COMES FREEDOM

When we began this project, we were reluctant to refer to the women of Cohort 25—or to ourselves—as "retired." The word seemed to embody many negative connotations of loss, diminishment, and the pulling back of energy. Yet, the more we talked with women, especially during the follow-up conversations a year later, the more we heard a reworking of the word "retired." Of course, the word itself was an accurate statement of the employment status of some women, but as the women of Cohort 25 extended it to include their own transformations and the lives they were leading after their careers, the word became richer, fuller. No longer a synonym for loss and decline, it became the setting for new ideas and energy. What so many women had feared—that admitting to being retired would result in their disappearance and a loss of meaning in their lives—turned out to be untrue. We could hear the change as they described their situations: "I may be retired from the corporate world, but I am not a *retired person*,"; "I am feeling a new sense of freedom and opportunity;" and "The world looks like a whole new place to me; I have dropped my old identity." One woman seemed to sum up the experiences of the cohort: "I am very happy with the decisions that have been made. I have gotten through a rough patch stronger and in a different place."

And when we asked, simply, "How are you?" the unanimity of the responses caught us off guard: "I'm good—busy!"; "I feel very content right now"; "I'm so busy, I can't even tell you ... all fun things have come my way"; and "I am currently happy with everything I'm doing."

COMING TO TERMS

"This part is considered old when you're young; when you're here, it's different."

In our follow-up conversations, we heard how women were coming to terms with an important part of themselves and their identity. The same strengths that had made them successful in their careers were allowing them to face the challenges of the transition to retirement as another hurdle they knew they could clear. Talking about their fears and sharing their experiences with one another had triggered the introspection they needed to go forward. In the past, the demands of their careers might not have allowed them much time for introspection, but when they could stop, reflect, and refocus their energies, they were able to become comfortable with things they found pleasure in outside the workplace: family and friendships, work—perhaps part-time or unpaid—and activities they truly enjoyed, not necessarily things they thought they *should* do.

Just as they broke new ground with each hurdle they cleared in their academic and professional advancement, they were breaking new ground once more as they changed their expectations about retirement. The women were confident and eager, just as they had been in their twenties. Each woman, in her own way, was realizing the potential she had to shape a life and an identity after her full-time career.

Many had moved past their postcareer uneasiness and the accompanying urge to immediately get busy with something new. Unscheduled time, that "big, floaty thing" one woman so accurately described in her interview, was not as disconcerting as it had first appeared. In fact, women were managing their time quite skillfully, taking on and committing to things that really mattered to them, often after a period of deliberate slowing down. They may not all have been writing the books they once imagined—although some certainly were—but they were exploring volunteer opportunities they never knew existed, giving back to their colleges and communities, and finding pleasure in living their lives as successfully in retirement as they had during their careers. What they were discovering was that they had the opportunity to tell a new or different story about what "retirement" could be. They were realizing that it was indeed up to them to change the expectations about the next stage of their lives. The women in this cohort were becoming the "firsts" once again.

NOTE

1. For more on the power of engaging with our passions and developing our potential in later life, see Mary Catherine Bateson, *Composing a Further Life: The Age of Active Wisdom* (New York: Vintage, 2011).

7

Why Are the Stories of Baby Boomer Women Important?

Whether it is because of self-consciousness or self-censorship, modesty or fear, many people do not easily tell their own stories. A woman who drew on her own experiences as a child to create conversation groups for immigrant families talked about the importance of giving people an opportunity to tell others about their experiences: "People have amazing stories and so often, they don't feel they should tell anyone." Individuals who might not have otherwise told their stories felt safe and welcomed in the environment she had created. In many ways, she could have been talking about the women of Cohort 25. They had amazing stories of their own and often told us they were revealing something about themselves that they had seldom, if ever, shared with anyone else. Yet it seemed as though they knew intuitively how important sharing their stories would be for themselves and for others. Countless times, when we asked women to expand on short answers from their surveys or when a focus group paused in its conversation, what they turned to were the stories they knew intimately, stories about themselves.

When we tell the stories of our lives, we bring our memories out into the open. We pass them on or set them down on paper for ourselves and others. Perhaps, in telling our stories, we see a truth or an irony we never noticed before. Perhaps we hope others—our spouses, partners, children, friends—will understand in a new way who we are, what we have experienced. The stories in this book are brief, often excerpts from interview sessions, but their ability to capture women's experiences is powerful.

Our research process offered women many opportunities to tell their stories, and although we had eagerly looked forward to hearing what they had to say, we soon learned that we weren't the only ones who were learning new things. Telling their stories opened the door to introspection and greater self-awareness on the part of the women themselves. We could not have anticipated for sure how the experience would affect them, but telling their stories allowed them to step back and consider their lives and careers from a broad perspective. They were able to select and present details in whatever manner they chose and to move seamlessly between past and present. Often, when they did so, the full impact of something long held in memory came into sharp relief.

The women's stories unfolded quite easily, as if waiting to be told. Indeed, much of the material in the previous chapters has been selected from the women's spontaneous personal narratives. Although we refer to these narratives as "stories," it is important to distinguish them from invented works of fiction and to think of them as deliberately told, personal accounts of how things happened and what the women felt. Sometimes, they spoke about the past and how their careers began; other times, they focused on the present moment, scrutinizing where exactly they stood as they made their way into retirement. When they presented the events of their lives through narratives, women told us in their own words what they had desired, where they had compromised, and where they hoped to travel, both literally and emotionally. Their stories added exponentially to our understanding of their lives and the complex truths that shaped them.

WHAT WAS IT LIKE?

"I think we have a unique past to talk about during a historic time, and we will create a new paradigm for older/younger women in the future." This woman's observation captured what is probably the biggest single appeal in the stories of Baby Boomer women—their unique view on history. They can tell us what it was like. Among the twenty-five women in this book, we have met many women who broke new ground in their professions or institutions. In their historical roles, often as "firsts," Baby Boomer women in general had intimate, first-hand knowledge of what it took to make change in the workplace. They felt both the flak and the pride that came with being a visible sign of change, often in offices and institutions that were not prepared to welcome them. For many, that meant regularly tuning out condescension or sexual innuendo. It meant maintaining focus and dealing with distractions large and small, personal and professional. The women of Cohort 25 understood that change was needed and that they were often going to be the ones caught at the critical point where old and new attitudes intersected.

Sometimes being the first wasn't the whole story. What it took to get there was the real story. One woman who was putting in an average of

110 hours a week, with no limits on her hours and no maternity leave, described what she faced when she hoped to take time off after the birth of her baby:

> I worked to combine my four weeks of allowed vacation and then asked for an additional two weeks of unpaid leave. The answer was *no*. When I found out that a male colleague was getting six weeks of paid leave for a ski injury, I challenged the response to my own request and was granted part of what I had asked for.

So many details in this anecdote made it dramatically clear that entering a previously male-dominated profession was just the first hurdle for women. Even after completing their undergraduate and graduate or professional education, women had to be resourceful to find work-around solutions and to negotiate. This woman had to ask and ask again for two weeks of *unpaid leave*. Beyond the demanding hours and the need to cobble together already limited vacation time, the eye-opening moment came when she learned a male colleague was being paid for time off. Young parents today will certainly appreciate the struggle to secure time off to be with their newborns, but the essential unfairness lying just beneath the surface is as disturbing now as it was thirty-plus years ago.

The back stories—the slow, steady effort to challenge policies, form alliances, and stay focused on long-term goals—were just some of the narratives women had to share. And we need to pay attention. The women interviewed for this book challenged practices and changed policies. They were test cases. They participated in and created pilot projects. They drove change throughout their careers, and their stories captured the immediacy of their experiences and the difficulties they encountered. What strategies and support were required to develop a university's first-date rape education program? Or to make it possible for a major international corporation to achieve a score of 100 percent on the Corporate Equity Index ranking of policies and practices affecting LGBT employees? These accomplishments—driven by the efforts of women in Cohort 25—were not just stories of corporate or institutional change; they were also stories of personal courage and commitment. Every professional Baby Boomer woman of the time has a story like this. If it wasn't she herself who spearheaded a specific effort, she knew of the people who did. Change was everywhere, in virtually every professional setting, and it affected individuals throughout organizations.

Woven among the inspiring stories we heard, there were also other, very different stories, sometimes just quick glimpses into experiences women mentioned in passing. These were the stories in which women were defeated, in which their ambitions were mocked or undermined. This example from one woman's longer reflection on her early professional influences stood out starkly when we knew she went on to have a long and successful career:

> My mother told me my grades weren't high enough for medical school. Now I know that probably wasn't true, but only one *no* was a killer for me. It was too easy to have a damper put on me.

Told in an almost offhand manner, this anecdote made a very important point. Although young women often heard the encouraging mantra "you can do anything you set your mind to," that wasn't the case in every family or for every young woman. Women were not automatically given unconditional encouragement, and some had to struggle within themselves to overcome the "dampers" and discouragements that threatened to kill their aspirations. This example helps us think about the impact of such discouragement in a way that data collected on women's medical school applications could never do. Other instances in which women's ambitions could easily have been tamped down —when the education of sons took precedence over that of daughters, or when a certain field of study or career was simply dismissed as inappropriate for a woman—were embedded in the stories of the women we interviewed.

The irony in another story provided a painful personal revelation that we would never discover if we looked only at statistics about women's participation in training programs. This woman was describing the behavior of a high-ranking officer in the international organization where she worked:

> Knowing I was going into a training program, he said, "You are the kind of woman who ruins men's lives, who backs men against walls and gets them to buy her gold and jewelry." And yet the same guy always praised me and rose to give me a standing ovation when I spoke.

A quick but telling anecdote, this little story captured not only the language of sexual harassment but also the hypocrisy women experienced as they advanced in their careers.

But these women kept going. They deflected or ignored the negative, undermining comments. They sought alternative paths and learned to be strategic early on. Their stories were filled with accounts of unshrinking, undeterred forward movement.

TELLING STORIES BECOMES A PROCESS OF DISCOVERY

Listening to themselves as they told their stories helped women pay closer attention to the significance of their own narratives. Sometimes, they heard their stories as if for the first time and were inspired: "The conversation I had with you got me thinking about what things meant to me and what I needed to do."

In other instances, women revisited their past and looked back at the origins of a memory from their childhood, as happened when a follow-up question led to a sweet and thought-provoking response. When we asked in the survey if there were a particular person(s) who influenced her professional interests and direction, one woman wrote in the name of a friend's mother. We followed up on this and asked her during the interview, "Could you tell us how she influenced you?" Her response was very revealing. She recalled the admiration she had felt as a child when she was fascinated by and looked up to her friend's mother. Her words were full of enthusiasm as she described the woman, but they were also tempered by her own experience as an adult.

She was a different kind of mom, a teacher and artist, who stayed up late. In fact, I now realize she may not have been a great mother, but she had a career she loved, and had other interests, such as fashion. I also used her marriage as a model, and it, too, may not have been so perfect.

Seen through the eyes of a young girl, this woman was breaking the norms of the 1950s mother. It may not have taken much more than simply being a little different, being herself, for the friend's mother to create a lasting impression and provide a model—even if it wasn't perfect—that inspired this woman to see more possibilities for herself and her life. In telling us this story, as an adult, the woman realized things she could not have known as a child. Nonetheless, the friend's mother remained in her memory, a symbol of possibility she had carried with her since childhood.

THE PERSPECTIVE THAT COMES FROM EXPERIENCE

Looking back at their lives by telling their stories, the women of Cohort 25 sometimes said they saw or heard things they hadn't realized before. This was the case with a woman we introduced earlier when she described the networking help her male classmate had been receiving: "He showed me a letter he was writing to an ad firm, saying that 'Mr. So-and-So' recommended he write to them. Somehow, I did not learn the lesson of that."

When we first shared this story, it was within the context of professional networking, to which women had very little access in the early years of their careers. When we look at it again and pay special attention to her use of the word "lesson," we can hear the woman herself realizing there was something significant that she didn't see at the time, the lesson that the male student was benefiting from and learning to use contacts and recommendations she was missing out on. This is just one instance in which, by telling their stories, women brought to the surface events and actions that might have passed unnoticed in their careers. They may not have fully realized the significance of an event or a conversation until decades later, perhaps when they began to tell the story to others, or when added years of maturity and experience made it impossible to miss the "lesson" in a situation.

LISTENING CAREFULLY

When women told their stories, we listened. We wanted to learn about their experiences and to understand how their unique place in history had shaped them. We wanted to give them the opportunity to talk to others and to reflect on the experiences they shared. But in addition to capturing facts and chronologies, we were paying close attention to the stories themselves and to the individual qualities of each woman's narrative. They were all different. The words the women chose and how they selected, ordered, emphasized, or downplayed events were all under their control. They were their own narrators, recounting their lives in their own voices. Ultimately, each woman took charge not only of how she told her story but also of how she wanted to talk about her future. Reflecting on the role women's personal narratives played in the transition process, two key elements come into focus: how they used language and how they structured their stories.

In earlier chapters, we described the connections among different women's experiences. However, when we listen to their individual stories, it is the qualities that distinguish them from one another that become meaningful. This is especially true in terms of their use of language. Women's descriptions of the events in their lives were often very vivid. Putting memories into words brought back intense emotions, and thinking about the future elicited a broad range of responses, from anticipation, to anxiety, to exuberance.

MAKING COMPARISONS

When women talked about their lives, they drew comparisons. Sometimes they borrowed familiar comparisons or figures of speech, and sometimes they created their own. Their language revealed aspects of their identity, how they saw themselves, and what was personally meaningful for them. Often the language they chose was active, with references to moving forward or outward. But sometimes their language also suggested a level of worry that could not be captured in the short answers of a survey instrument.

When women used nonliteral language, their comparisons were often clever and funny. A sly turn of phrase could capture the uncomfortable essence of a new responsibility, as in this comment, about being a role model for the next generation: "These big girl shoes hurt!"

Descriptive language could also be blunt and frank. One woman, who regularly faced draining litigious conflicts in her work, told how she drew on her previous counseling experience, when "I was thrown in and had to claw my way."

And here, another woman's use of metaphor conveyed a remarkable tenderness and sense of responsibility when she was talking about the role of caregiver: "We don't want to become resentful of those we are caring for and have it seep into the fiber of the person who needs us."

Each of these examples demonstrates the power of women's language to capture and convey passionate, intuitive responses. Our research instruments were detailed and thorough and very effective in collecting data about the lives of women in Cohort 25, but the personal, human concerns of their individual lives came through most profoundly in their interactions with us and with one another. Our understanding of their lives was enriched and made more complete by listening to what they said and how they said it. It was through their own words that we heard unfiltered emotions, empathy, and, sometimes, long-held resentments.

When we contacted the women a year after our first interviews and asked how they were doing, most of them had moved well into the process of transition. Their language was richly descriptive. Many used comparisons to active, mechanical processes to describe what was going on in their lives. Even if they were devoting large amounts of time to their home or family, they did not make comparisons usually associated with domesticity or nurturing. Instead, more than anything, the comparisons women used to describe their lives referred to active, deliberate *movement*.

Some of the metaphors were mechanical; some were taken from music or from nature. One woman said she was "recalibrating" all the time. She felt very lucky to have professional assignments that called on her to tap into the creativity she loved and to solve complicated problems. Another woman used the same metaphor of "calibrating" to describe time she had spent adjusting and taking external factors into account when making decisions. She spoke of feeling her way around. After joining several boards, she engaged in an active process of learning about the structure of various organizations and determining what her role might be: "I am figuring out how I want to *calibrate* myself in this way."

And here, a related metaphor captures the sense of deliberateness as another speaker described how she was assessing her life: "It's a *measuring* time; I let myself down on projects I'd wanted, but life has its demands."

Other figures of speech the women used were kinesthetic, capturing the energy they were feeling as they moved into a new part of their lives, as in "I am finding a *new rhythm*" or "*I have parted the waves* and made room for projects I wanted to work on."

They did not see their lives as static or quiet. Instead, they were actively seeking new things, eager for what was next. Adjusting, moving, figuring things out: qualities the women of Cohort 25 had used to describe their careers from the beginning were still characterizing their lives as they made the transition to retirement.

Women also used figurative language that deliberately pointed out the premium they were placing on time. One woman turned to language evocative of death, coining a figure of speech reminiscent of loss, both the loss of fertility and loss in a chess game: "*The death clock is ticking*, just like the biological clock. Life is finite, and there's an *endgame*." She used this extended metaphor as an incentive, saying, "You don't have endless amounts of time; if you're gonna do it, you better do it now."

Another woman who had experienced both the serious illness and difficult divorce of family members since her retirement said she was appreciating the "time above the line," having the inevitable sense that things could change. "I've seen enough to know the shoe will drop," she said. The phrase "time above the line" has applications in many professional areas, including accounting, marketing, leadership, and education. Here, it suggests time spent in conscious, thoughtful behavior, time before the shoe dropped and everything changed.

FOR EACH WOMAN, HER OWN STYLE

Another aspect of women's stories that could not be conveyed by surveys was how they organized and narrated events. In telling their stories, the women of Cohort 25 were free to emphasize or even withhold whatever they liked. They knew their stories better than anyone, so they could narrate them as they liked, perhaps adding drama or conflict or a lesson. The most important aspect of the women's narrative style was that it put the women themselves in charge of how their stories were told, and in doing so, it helped us understand what they considered important and how they saw themselves.

Just as each woman in Cohort 25 had her own lexicon of descriptive language, each also had a personal style when it came to narrating the events of her life. As women talked to us, they remembered, organized, and narrated the details of their past actions and decisions. They put the parts together in patterns that worked best and seemed natural for them. They moved with ease through the material of their lives, simultaneously looking back over the length of their careers and projecting forward into the years ahead.

Many women described the events of their lives as unfolding in a linear pattern, as if following a timeline. One event or accomplishment led to another. A decision or a relationship resulted in the next step: "I met my future husband in October, was engaged by Christmas, and got married one week after finishing my master's."

Women often used a linear approach when they talked about how they arrived at big decisions or how they followed a course of action that seemed logical, even inevitable, at the time. They focused on the chronological order of events in their lives and often referred to the influence their parents, partners, or spouses had on those events.

A second approach was entirely different, when women stressed their willingness to be open to the unexpected and to take risks. They spoke about making leaps into the unknown and described serendipitous encounters in which luck sometimes played a key role. Often, women used this approach when talking about the decision to make an unlikely career move. Perhaps it meant turning their interests in a brand-new direction or striking out on their own—sometimes against the strong advice of others—without knowing where the decision might lead. One woman who had made many career moves described the process of her advancement with these words: "People would say, 'are you interested in doing something different?' and I would think, 'it will be at least a year before they find out I don't know what I'm doing . . .'"

In other instances, women told their stories in a way that emphasized the role of self-awareness. They recognized the importance of their own effort and agency in shaping their careers, especially when it came to deliberate, strategic preparation. The steps moving forward were the direct result of that preparation.

> A mentor helped me see the value of keeping myself open when I was successful and looking for "what's next." I was able to take risks because I had security based on previous work and pension plans. I knew how to manage money and knew what I needed and wanted.

These patterns are, at best, broad generalizations, and people use or adapt different styles at different times. As Baby Boomers simultaneously look in two directions, back on our careers and ahead, toward the future, paying attention to how we each tell our own stories can have benefits for us as well as others. Not only will our friends and family members learn more about us, but we can also listen to our own stories, alert to the language and structures we use as we form the unwieldy jumble of memories, plans, and dreams into a coherent storyline.

What kinds of language do we use to describe ourselves and our actions, both as our earlier selves and as the people we are in the process of becoming, our postcareer selves?

How do we structure our stories? Do we like to think of each step as the logical extension of earlier decisions and commitments? A welcomed opportunity for new adventures? Maybe the events in our lives are framed by our careful planning and self-knowledge? Or, maybe, it is none of these, but instead, our own personally crafted narrative model by which we hold on to and share our stories.

The women in Cohort 25 used language as a critical tool in their postcareer self-reflection. They typed out responses, answered questions in detail, and engaged several times with us and with each other. The rigor and felicity with which they expressed themselves demonstrated just how important it was for them to "get it right," to make themselves clear, and to verbalize their experiences in ways that felt accurate and true. They took language seriously. Because of this, their stories possessed an immediacy that can never be brought to life by data. Their voices too, captured in their own words and style, were the product of the era and the education that shaped them. They were articulate and nuanced in their speech, with a confidence that served them well. They also understood the power of irony and humor, as we heard when a woman from Cohort 25 seized on the perfect adjective to describe the combination of courage and practicality that drove her forward in the early years of her career. As she said, simply, "I had *gumption.*"

8

What Are the Lessons We Can All Take Away?

The women in Cohort 25 were candid and generous with us. They gave us unique access to information about their families, their lives, and their careers. They shared with us the experiences that shaped them and the things they learned along the way. As we step back and view their contributions to our research as a small sample of individual lives isolated from the broader panorama of their generation, we can see that there were not only important individual differences, but there were also numerous qualities the women had in common and shared with other Baby Boomers. If we pay close attention, we see that several shared personal characteristics and experiences rise to the surface, stark and inarguable. Patterns also emerge in how the women talked about the future and what made them happy. From the overlapping qualities the women had in common, we have drawn lessons we hope will be useful to others. Beyond the particulars of any individual woman's life, what message can readers take away? What lessons are there in the experiences of the women of Cohort 25?

YOUR STORIES MATTER: TELL THEM

As we have seen, the narratives of the women of Cohort 25 had a unique power to engage the imaginations of others and to bring others into a time and place where women's lives and opportunities were constantly changing. The power of stories to celebrate, reveal, and connect can be astonishing. Stories can also move others to action. They can offer firsthand evidence of how far women have come and how far they have yet to go.

By listening to women's stories, we gained information we would never have been able to find through other sources. The women, too, benefited from telling their stories, a point they made many times. Based upon these experiences, our advice to others, especially Baby

Boomer women, is to tell your stories and write them down. Whether you are preserving a personal history for yourself and your family or hoping to publish a memoir, your stories need to be told. Your stories recall the experiences of a particular period in time, told from your unique point of view. As culture and values and opportunities change, your stories will serve as a benchmark against which change, however fast or slow, may be measured. Regardless of the words or structure of any particular woman's story, what matters is that you remember, record, and pass on the stories of the life you have lived.

YOUR PROFESSIONAL LIFE AND ACCOMPLISHMENTS WILL ALWAYS BE PART OF WHO YOU ARE

Becoming professionals changed women. It changed how they saw themselves and what they knew they were capable of. They brought to the workplace new ideas about women's qualifications and drive, about gender equality, and about how the workplace itself could be improved by the presence of women. As they embarked on their careers, they joined and contributed to diverse groups of men and women working together. They came to use the word "colleague" to refer to a kind of relationship far fewer women of earlier generations had ever experienced. It was a word that embodied the commitment they had made to working with and alongside others, in professions often characterized by their own cultures and specialized language.

For the first time, too, it became easier for women to rise to positions of leadership in their fields. They thrived in environments where they were rewarded for teamwork and innovation. They took on the responsibilities of leading organizations, influencing the careers of others, setting policy, and serving as the public face for major institutions. Often, they were looked up to, admired, emulated, and, at other times, criticized, ignored, or marginalized.

Taken together, how do these experiences from women's working lives best serve them after their careers? In interviews and in groups, the women of Cohort 25 were emphatic: they were very uncomfortable saying "I used to be a ..." when referring to the career they had left. And then, often, they described how they were continuing to use the skills and strategies of their careers in new ways. As much as women spoke about leaving titles and business cards behind, it became clear from our conversations that their professional lives were inextricably part of who they would always be.

Just as their family background and childhood influences were woven into their personalities and values, likewise, the culture and demands of their chosen professions had shaped them. How they approached problems, what they thought of as success, and how they interacted with others were all influenced by the professional environments where they established themselves and built careers. For decades, women spent the majority of their time thinking, problem solving, and using the language of their professions. Whether they were professors or corporate executives, artists or physicians, their professional identities were intertwined with their personal identities. At the same time, they shaped and had a lasting impact on the professions in which they worked, so the influence was not all in one direction. The best parts, though, and the parts they continued to value and hold on to, were the things they loved most about their careers.

HOLD ON TO THE BEST PARTS

What piqued your curiosity and passion when you were starting out? What convinced you that a certain career was right for you, the best fit, the best use of your talents? What kept you growing and learning? Those fundamental elements will always be part of you. It may be a love of numbers and the satisfaction that comes from solving a complex equation. Or perhaps it is the innate ability to take charge and lead others, to recognize good ideas and know how to advance them. Is it confidence in being able to use language effectively, or the deep engagement of hours spent in research? Being able to help others feel better about themselves? Being able to design and create something beautiful? Each person we spoke to was passionate about some fundamental aspect of her profession. These were the basic, elemental qualities of their careers: the qualities that first attracted them to a given profession. How their love of numbers, language, or art, or their desire to help other people, could be put to use professionally grew in depth and sophistication as their careers went forward, but the fundamental attraction and satisfactions remained. These "best parts" of a career can find new expression and be the drivers for exploration far beyond our full-time careers.

In particular, the creativity women cited as one of the things they most enjoyed during their careers was still central. As the women of Cohort 25 talked about what they were doing after retirement, the creativity quotient was a big factor. The challenge of taking on a new project invigorated women and often gave them an opportunity to reapply, rediscover, or completely repurpose skills and expertise they had developed in their careers. This was the case with the entrepreneur who spent years working for a large corporation and then built her own business and created jobs for others. When she left the corporate world, her first project was to turn her energy to gutting and completely remodeling a house.

As you look back and isolate the "best parts" of your own professional life, here are some things to think about:

What empowered you?
What motivated you?
When did you feel competent? Appreciated?
How did you know when you had a "good fit" with the organization?
What challenged you?

Also, consider what were the day-to-day tasks (e.g., research, public speaking, designing, helping others, teaching, facilitating, coaching, writing, building, advocacy, problem solving, organizing) that you most enjoyed? The pleasure and accomplishments that accrued from the tasks you enjoyed and were good at can serve as building blocks for your activities and thoughtful engagement in the future.

After a long career in academic administration, one woman looked back and described the tactics she used when she faced new projects in her work: "Convene. Generate ideas. Move ahead. These constituted my authority when I was working." Rather than abandon those successful and satisfying strategies after retiring, she found new ways to apply by bringing the same purposeful approaches to active community engagement.

KEEP WORKING WITH OTHERS

Not one woman in Cohort 25 celebrated the *solitude* of retirement. Some described the initial need to decompress, to be quiet and reflective for a while after first leaving their full-time careers. And others described the pleasures of a less scheduled, less hectic life; but to a person, they emphasized the satisfactions and excitement of continuing to *work with* others, whether that work took the form of part-time employment, philanthropic activities, volunteering for a nonprofit agency, mentoring, or serving on a board. They did not talk about the prestige of holding a position or having a seat at the table. Instead, they spoke of action. When they described being involved with others, they chose much the same language they had used when describing their careers. They brought knowledge and expertise and concern for others to this new work. They figured out how to calibrate their skills and leadership strengths to new roles. They wanted to give their best, to fit in, and to be respected.

In women's conversations about staying involved, we can detect strong, if unstated, views about work itself. The women of Cohort 25 spent their adult lives striving for and earning professional status. They worked within settings in which they were required to invest their time, energy, and, sometimes, even identities, in the culture of an institution, a corporation, or even their own businesses. They understood in their bones what it took to give of themselves to make something successful. The willingness to invest themselves in this way did not evaporate with retirement, but rather, it became more sharpened and focused. In retirement, they could be selective in where they placed their energies, but they were no less interested in and excited by opportunities to work on projects that required serious effort and on which they could regularly interact and collaborate with others.

The benefits to be gained from this continuing commitment to working with others are enormous: the pleasure of knowing you are part of a group and contributing to an effort that matters and the satisfaction of knowing that you are appreciated for who you are, what you have done, and what you have to give. There are also the benefits of keeping up your skills of listening, critical thinking, and compromise, and of valuing the mutual respect that comes from working with others who have diverse backgrounds and perspectives.

REACH OUT AND CREATE NEW NETWORKS

Your world can suddenly seem much smaller when you are no longer going each day to an office filled with people you know or when the ready-made relationships of your profession are not there to provide the contacts or collegial guidance you need to adjust to a new way of life. This is the time to borrow the best from your professional experience in making contacts and nurturing relationships. Become the bright center of your own new and growing network. Many women speak of reaching out to old friends and reestablishing relationships that had slipped away. Others emphasize the need to forge new relationships, to extend themselves and get to know strangers with the same openness and curiosity as if they had recently transferred to a new community. Even if you have not moved to a new city, the challenge of establishing new acquaintances and introducing those acquaintances to one another can be stimulating and daunting at the same time.

We asked a woman whose career had spanned law, publishing, and writing, and who had continued to work part-time for several years after her retirement, how she was doing during the first year when she felt she no longer had a schedule. She replied, "Good," adding that she was exploring a new exercise program. However, it turned out that the benefits of the program were more than physical health, as the routine had given her the opportunity to connect with others: "For me, to even sound upbeat at this time of the year is unusual. It's a tough time with the lack of light. Exercise is also a new channel to meet new people."

From the women who had traveled widely during their careers, we heard a special emphasis on the importance of building networks. Some had made international moves that had a lasting impact on their personal and professional lives. Some continued to have strong, permanent international connections, with family and friends in Europe, Africa, and the United States. When we asked an open-ended question about what they were doing, the answers were surprisingly similar. After raising the possibility that she might relocate, one of the women talked about the things that had not changed for her and also things that had been new for her in the previous year: "The 501C3 [nonprofit, tax-exempt organization] I am involved with is the same, as is the University board I serve on. I am building a new network in Paris for the University." Another woman described being part of an effort to organize and mobilize an international group of influential and experienced women:

> All of the women are Americans, but some live in Paris. They are now sharing experiences, finding out how to handle business and overseas life. It's an exchange and support group; the network is just beginning to develop. I have had one telephone meeting with them—it's very exciting!

As you build a new network, whether you connect through conversation at the gym or by a transatlantic call, the important thing is to bring people into your circle to share the projects, activities, or concerns that are important to you. Find out what you don't know about your community and the institutions you might have been too busy to investigate when you were working full-time. Meet others; ask questions. And talk about what is important to you.

Again and again, the women of Cohort 25 enthusiastically spoke of the value of talking, formulating their thoughts, saying things out loud, and knowing they were being heard. What they universally celebrated throughout the research was the pleasure and importance of talking to us and to one another. They found common experiences and joked about fears or insecurities they shared.

As you enter a new, unfamiliar era after your full-time career, the sense of a shared past, of common ground, can be established by reaching out not only to friends or colleagues but also to others in the community, individuals you meet through common interests, volunteering, or social organizations. Like good colleagues from your career, new contacts from outside your familiar sphere can help point to the way ahead, advising you about what to look for and what to avoid.

CURATE YOUR CONTRIBUTIONS

For years, women negotiated difficult exchanges of time, energy, and financial resources. Where could they best invest the resources they had at their disposal? They understood very well the multiple demands their careers placed upon them, daily, monthly, yearly, and that is where they invested a great deal of time and talent. Financially, they might have had the resources to contribute to causes they embraced and to support projects beyond the walls of their home and offices, without necessarily having time to become directly involved. With the demands and constraints of their careers lifted, the women of Cohort 25 had more freedom to decide what and how they would give to others. Some described engaging in an inventory-like process in which they took stock of what they had to give and how and where they would contribute their expertise, time, and money. Most would have agreed that the contributions they chose to make in retirement could provide a fundamental sense of satisfaction and identity, but those contributions, regardless of the currency, were all finite in their own way.

Based on the experiences of many of the women, taking your time and choosing wisely are essential steps in ensuring that you will be content with your contributions, whatever their form. Be mindful, shrewd, flexible, and creative as you commit yourself and your resources. Several women described the experience of getting into and later getting out of a commitment that seemed at first to be a perfect fit.

As we listened to women's accounts of how they reviewed, selected, adopted, and changed their commitments, the verb that seemed to best fit the process was "curate." Just as gallery directors make critical selections when they are choosing works of art that will complement one another, or as social media experts recommend curating one's online profile, the lesson we can draw from women's experiences is that you must carefully *curate* the obligations you make to others, whether individuals or organizations. One woman added another key component in the decisions she made to give of her time, saying, "My efforts to diversify in volunteering turned out to be necessary."

Diversify; try other things. Put together a curated package of what works best for you and where you wish to put your energy. Of necessity, too, the choices that seem to be the best fit during the first year after a person's retirement most likely will need to be adjusted in one or two or ten years. The board that seemed like the ideal venue for your professional interests may be less satisfying when your role becomes entirely one of fundraising. Or the committee where you thought you could add value to the deliberations may not acknowledge your input for reasons you are not really privy to, such as their internal conflicts or style or personality differences. What do you do? Move on. Look for other options. Maybe it is wise to place less emphasis on seeking volunteer activities that directly align with your professional expertise. Or maybe the skills you honed in your career can be more satisfactorily applied in a new setting you were not even aware of when you first retired.

MAKE FRIENDS WITH TIME

Hectic, fully scheduled days spent in a career run into one another, and years can slide into decades almost before we know it. With retirement, we have the opportunity to take some control over those days, to take charge of time. Yet for many women, other commitments seemed poised to fill the vacuum created when they step out of their careers. Women seemed happiest when they were taking charge of time, making a plan, even when that plan was easily subject to change. Sometimes that meant slowing down, doing some exploring, not rushing from one heavily committed way of life to another. "Have patience with life" were the reassuring words we heard from one woman.

Many of the women talked about setting aside something "for themselves." They spoke of time carved out of busy weeks that would allow them to focus on an activity that was personally important to them. Whether it was physical activity—from workout sessions to golf—reading, meditation, a religious service, spiritual exploration, or a combination of things, they made sure it was there. Valuing this time as a commitment to yourself, as something you need to have, a commitment that makes you a better person, adds an element of mindfulness and focus that many women considered essential to their lives and their well-being.

Another woman and her husband had to work out many arrangements after he retired and then went back to work again at a brand-new position: "We have become very flexible. . . . This is very calming, but in my forties or fifties, I would have been a wreck. Flexibility seems to be the key." When the same woman described consulting with her daughter and son-in-law on their new business, she again mentioned flexibility and "taking things as they come." It is probably not a word often used to characterize the retirement of her parents' generation, but as she described it, remaining "flexible"—being adaptive and strategic, as that word suggests—was key to her sense of well-being.

RECOGNIZE THAT YOUR DECISIONS ARE SHAPED BY RELATIONSHIPS

Certainly women of Cohort 25 developed and valued a strong sense of self and independence that carried them through their careers and sustained them in making tough decisions, taking a stand when necessary, and moving ahead. But there is no getting around it: for virtually all of the women in Cohort 25, that independence coexisted with a powerful interdependence. The dynamics of the relationships they had with other people affected their lives from every conceivable perspective. When they talked about their lives, they also talked about their spouses, their longtime partners, their elderly parents, dependent children, grandchildren, sisters, brothers, great-aunts, and friends. Retirement may have freed them from the demands of their careers and changed how they saw themselves, but the responsibilities and pleasures created by their attachments to others certainly endured after women left the workplace. When we acknowledge the role of relationships—perhaps much more complex in retirement than it was earlier in our lives—we are better able to sort out our responses and responsibilities, to set limits and be realistic.

FIND THE ENERGY IN CHANGE

We have seen how rapid and continual changes in technology have completely remade the workplace, just as the social and political environments around us continue to change. Change itself can be invigorating or threatening. Baby Boomer women successfully navigated change at home and in the workplace throughout their careers. How can people who often saw themselves as agents for change in their professions and in the workplace respond to the changes that inevitably accompany their retirement? In fact, the women in Cohort 25 developed an arsenal of strategies that helped them deal with change.

They learned to size up a situation, to do the necessary research, and to improvise, dig in, and push on. They also learned to trust their intuition and their strengths, and most importantly, they learned to stay connected and to thrive.

The women of Cohort 25 taught us by example that retirement is not a time for complacency. They described being energized by creating new spaces, moving to new locations, and renovating their homes. Remodeling and redecorating brought observable changes in light and color, but women also experienced other, less obvious, but perhaps more profound changes in ideas and perspective when they reimagined where and how they would live their lives in this new stage. *A transcontinental move to be near family members? A short-term condo rental for part of the year? Renting until we decide where to settle?*

For the women of Cohort 25, change arrived, too, in the form of new and evolving relationships and, inevitably, in personal loss. With each change in personal relationships, women were asked to define themselves again: they became grandparents, great-aunts, mothers-in-law. Perhaps they got married, or divorced, or their spouse or a parent died. How women took on these changes, how they squared off with the challenges they faced, was in many ways reminiscent of how they had faced change throughout their careers. They reacted, pivoted, if necessary, regrouped, and went on. Women described being energized by change they could control and also taking charge when change was forced upon them. They were not passive, and though some kinds of change were much more welcome than others, women repeatedly demonstrated the ability to find something invigorating or inspiring in changes that might have seemed daunting at first, such as a spouse's disability or the diagnosis of a serious illness.

DON'T STOP PUSHING FOR CHANGE

Many women enthusiastically described their early political involvement and embrace of feminism. Others made it clear they were not politically active during their college years, with some emphasizing that they were consumed by their need to work and establish their careers. However, more universally, the women talked about the experience of working on behalf of others *during their careers*. As we have seen, they made commitments across the board: from advocating for equity in the workplace, to job development for high-risk populations, to changes in the assessment of handicapped children.

Advocating for change played a significant role in the careers of many women in Cohort 25. The goal behind much of the work women were taking on after their careers was to help others. They often spoke of a renewed commitment to advocacy on behalf of their children and grandchildren. For years, this generation knew how to move an agenda forward, and many women told us they were finding a new kind of fulfillment in supporting individuals and causes they felt passionate about. Women were also continuing to lead by example, becoming politically active, mentoring young women coming up in their profession, and working with widows from the 9/11 attacks.

CONFIDENCE AND DETERMINATION ARE MORE IMPORTANT THAN EVER

The women of Cohort 25 jumped in and figured out what it would take to be successful as they advanced professionally. Sometimes, they made that leap without knowing where it would lead. The job was brand new; the expectations were unclear. The same may be said of their future after retirement. Women were continuing to take leaps of all kinds without always knowing where they would land: building a house, moving to a new city, starting a business, teaching a course for the first time. The confidence and determination that drove this generation into the workplace had not disappeared. If anything, women appeared to have a gathering sense of the increased importance of taking charge and staying involved.

They were speaking out, joining advocacy groups, and making their voices heard. They were driven by a sense of responsibility not only for themselves but also for future generations. They were modeling for the generations that would follow them—especially younger women, daughters, and granddaughters—the importance of getting involved.

FIND THE FREEDOM IN ASSERTING A NEW IDENTITY

Just as your identity changed with every new step in your life— when you graduated from college, advanced to a new position, entered a relationship, or had a child—now, with retirement, you are moving forward again and once more becoming the next version of yourself. This new stage encourages you to move into a new, positive identity. Accept and assert your identity as a vital, engaged person who *happens to be retired*—but only from a full-time career.

How does that new identity emerge and take shape? If you are not dressing for work and leaving for your office or lab or studio each day, how, in the words of T. S. Eliot, do you "prepare a face to meet the faces that you meet"?[1] How can we enjoy the greater flexibility and opportunities offered by retirement without feeling that we are losing our edge? How do we embrace a new identity without yielding to the smiling, gray-haired stereotypes presented in ads for retirement communities? One woman, still working for a national organization, described how her identity has already begun to change. She spoke of "getting bold" and feeling free to be more of herself at work, to dress less conservatively, and be more open with her coworkers. Her happiness at these changes suggests that she has already begun to experiment with seeing herself in a new way, preparing for new opportunities.

The lesson from the women in Cohort 25 comes through loud and clear: Keep being the person you always were, but be mindful and creative as you take on the evolution to your next stage. Take time to think back over the qualities that distinguished you as a professional, the skills, talents, and interests you always brought to the table. Think, too, about the things you had to set aside during your professional life or those things you omitted when you were asked to describe yourself. As we have seen, women in Cohort 25 were finding many ways to reconnect with causes and personal commitments they had not had time for during the years devoted to their careers. Ask yourself, *what did I set aside? What do I want to go back to now?* How can you now recover the essence of an idea or a commitment that was once your passion?

The answer is highly individual, but for many women, it involved an active recombining of personal qualities. Take the best parts of who you are and what you have done and been in the past, and use those as a starting point to explore what it is you are really interested in and how you want to live now. Perhaps the pieces appear disparate at first: time spent living in another culture, a college course that shaped your thinking in profound ways, the desire to learn more about your family history. You are no longer bound by the chronology or level of mastery or the achievements of your past endeavors. Instead, you are free to reorganize the pieces into a new composite. One woman described literally writing a new profile for herself, selecting, emphasizing, and reorganizing aspects of her life in an effort to describe the person she had become after leaving her career. When the professional template of our careers is lifted, what remains is a rich, complex history. Be curious. Look at what you have, and think about what you want to be.

We deliberately chose not to rank the dozen or so "lessons" in this chapter. Our goal was not to lay out a template or a checklist for all readers to follow. Rising as they do from the experiences of the women in Cohort 25, the lessons all have equal validity, so they are not ranked in a progression or hierarchy. We fully expect that some of the lessons will resonate much more profoundly than others with each individual, according to each person's experiences and personality. What we do hope this chapter provides is the encouragement to be open to what lies ahead and at the same time to be confident and emboldened as you take charge and make the future your own.

NOTE

1. T. S. Eliot, "The Love Song of J. Alfred Prufrock," in *The Complete Poems and Plays 1909–1950* (New York: Harcourt, Brace & World, 1934), 4.

9

Postcareer but *Future*-Oriented

The women of Cohort 25 were change agents throughout their adult lives. They were born in a time of growing prosperity and welcomed by parents who believed in the power of education, even as their families sometimes struggled out of poverty. Regardless of the circumstances of their birth and girlhoods, they rose to positions of success and privilege. They were told they could do anything they set their mind to. Hard work, focus, good humor, and luck all carried them forward. Along the way, the barriers against women's equal treatment began to fall. These Baby Boomers challenged the status quo of the workplace they entered; they worked around the impediments to their success; they persevered. Why wouldn't the drive that kept them going continue to motivate them as they once more strode into new territory?

When we came to know them during the period of our research, we were struck by their insistence on looking ahead. The Baby Boomer professional women of Cohort 25 were approaching the years after their full-time careers with a commitment to personal growth and exploration. The old norms simply did not apply. The idea that life after a career would be spent replicating the kind of retirement they observed when they were growing up struck these women as unimaginable. The generations of their grandparents, and later their parents, often welcomed retirement as a time to let go of responsibilities, to step back and settle into a quieter, nonworking life. As teenagers, the women of Cohort 25 already knew they wanted more than the traditional roles that had been open to women. In retirement, bolstered by the self-assurance and savvy they had gained from decades-long careers, they were again turning away from a conventional option that appeared far too limiting and outmoded. Rather than look to retirement as a long, contentment-filled vacation, they were imagining more numerous and more interesting opportunities for themselves. The women of Cohort 25 were excited about the future, and they recognized that their choices and attitudes would play a big part in changing what others saw as the possibilities for life after a full-time career.

After describing the success of a program she inaugurated for the mental health facility where she worked part-time, one woman summed up the benefits *she* gained from creating a program to help others: "I have a new sense of purpose, both professionally and personally."

Another woman, when we first met her, was happy in retirement but candid about looking for "something more," declaring, "I still have a lot in me." In the months that followed, she found a way to bring together her skills and love of teaching and turn her passion for canasta into a business. While teaching canasta privately and at adult education venues, she created a business selling starter kits that included everything a canasta player would need. The success of this 360-degree turn that converted a hobby into a successful business venture was thrilling for her. She described it as a "great step forward" and said, "I'm actually doing quite well with this new passion." Her success was a model for others, an example of taking the time to explore a passion, considering how it might be given a new form, and with creativity, taking it in a direction she had never imagined.

We have seen where these women came from and how they entered careers, took risks, and forged ahead as times and opportunities changed. Their apprehension about leaving those careers was greatly alleviated by talking with others and by the reality of what they encountered beyond the workplace. In our follow-up conversation, a lawyer showed how talking with others could be both stimulating and disconcerting:

> I have also been seeking out different people to talk to outside my business and professional network and experimenting more. I haven't talked to a single person who isn't happy. They are all traveling, taking courses, but there's nothing that's "wow, really?!" to me.

For her, the happiness of others was palpable, but instead of making her yearn for a trip or course she wanted to take, these conversations inspired her to look hard at a completely different option for her future. She was weighing the possibility of starting over and studying to be an engineer. Just the idea of pushing ahead and developing an aptitude she had had years earlier was energizing. "It gave me a skip in my step," she said.

She continued this reflection by suggesting that her experience in considering a new path was part of the message of this book. "If we do develop our latent interests and skills, who knows how we can use them?" Again, she was taking an assertively forward-looking stance. The point of her comment was not so much about whether she or any other Baby Boomer would complete an advanced degree in another field as it was about the sense of potential in how a re-invigorated cadre of Baby Boomer professionals might put their talents to use in new ways.

The women of Cohort 25 were realizing that they had an opportunity to discover who they were becoming at a new point in their lives —not just a "retired version of me" but a new engaged, assertive, and interesting "me" who happened to be retired. Just as they had welcomed other opportunities so many times during their lives, they were seizing this one, too.

Cultural changes that took place early in their careers presaged this shift. Doors opened to opportunity; laws changed; girls were told that with education they could do anything they set their minds to. As they moved into retirement, the open vista of possibilities referred not to professional advancement and all its perks but to personal advancement; once again, anything seemed possible. As the women of Cohort 25 began to enter the next stage of their lives, fortified with a new sense of purpose but free of many of the constraints of their careers, they were poised to make a difference. We are confident that the forward-looking lessons we distilled from the women of Cohort 25 will lead others to see themselves and their futures differently. What will be their impact on society if the emphasis in the lives of retired Baby Boomers shifts from "postcareer" to "future-oriented"?

The women of Cohort 25 were in their early sixties to early seventies when we conducted the follow-up phone calls. With the likelihood of a longer life expectancy than past generations, they could anticipate having twenty to thirty years ahead of them—a period easily equal to the amount of time they spent in their careers. How they would use those years and how they would combine the essence of their character and personalities with the best parts of their professional lives would define the role they continued to play in our culture. It would also make a difference in what the generations following the Baby Boomers came to expect for *themselves.*

The experiences of the women in Cohort 25 were similar to those of thousands of other individuals who were or would soon be leaving full-time careers. At the time when we followed up with one woman, she was serving on her 50th Reunion Committee. She described her high school classmates this way: "Everyone is still very active and looking for a meaningful way to live their life, without the obligation of going in to work every day." In her words, we heard something quite revealing. What her friends were looking for, "a meaningful way to live their life," now existed *outside* their careers. At age sixty-eight or so, they had left behind the obligations of their careers and were free to seek another way of life. Exchanging "going into work" for "living their life" signaled an exciting optimism about the next stage of their lives. If paying deliberate attention to how we live our lives takes on new emphasis in retirement, the results for ourselves and others can be dramatic. Greater self-awareness, combined with a concern for others and a commitment to make use of the best of our professional experiences, can be the formula for transformation, where deliberate attention to life after one's full-time career has the potential to bring a new level of engagement and enjoyment.

Placing more emphasis on the importance of a meaningful life is just one way that Baby Boomers will bring change to the postcareer years. What else are they bringing with them? If we return to Cohort 25, we realize how much they were influenced by the combination of values and attitudes they held in common and their longtime participation in the workplace. As a result, the women had internalized a powerful, shared culture.It is this internalized culture that prepared them to be future-oriented in retirement.

ENERGIZED BY A SENSE OF COMMON GROUND

When we look back at their individual profiles, the differences among the women of Cohort 25, specifically where they came from and what they brought to the workplace as young women, were quite profound. We created the mythical, composite profile that follows, comprising twenty-five statements from the twenty-five women, to illustrate just how far they all traveled to find this common ground.

My parents met in Siberia, where they were both in labor camps. My mother and father were very hard-working farmers. My father was a surgeon with an oil company in Palestine. My father was head of the music department, chaplain, and a pastor at an all-black, land grant college. My mother had wanted to work, but my father was dead set against it. I was always the bossy, curious child. I taught sailing since I was sixteen and went to an all-women's college. I saw school as a prison and couldn't wait to get out. I was good in athletics and had thought I would be a physical education teacher. I made films while in high school as an independent study. The military schools I attended until high school were all integrated; only when I went to public school in Florida did I encounter segregation. My mother took me to a vocational counselor who said I should be a physical therapist. I never knew what I was going to be when I grew up. I always loved teaching and *wanted* to teach. In my heart of hearts, I always wanted to be a psychologist. I always wanted to go to college, but it was out of the question since I had four brothers who

had to be educated. I left my hometown at seventeen and lived on a kibbutz in Israel for five years. I was the first in my family to go to college. It
was clear that I should find a career that was practical and where there
were a lot of jobs. I was gay and emerging from the closet, so I got very
caught up in following news about the feminist movement. My mother
was most influential and adamant that I have a career other than art.
When I got married, my husband told me it was time to get rid of my
blonde hair—it was not good for business. I did not have a female mentor until 1987. I was once told I was ambitious. I like the feeling that there
is always a path that might open new opportunities.

As we have learned, the women of Cohort 25 certainly did decide
what they wanted to do. They took on careers, and they took on the
workplace. When they met one another near the end of their careers,
their differences rapidly fell away. *They found common ground.* Despite
the differences in their backgrounds and life stories, they experienced
a sense of empowerment as a group. As they spoke with one another,
a rigorous sense of a shared identity emerged. That identity—as smart,
independent women who still wanted to be involved, still wanted to
give to others—transcended their individual differences. These Baby
Boomer career women were thriving and moving on from their full-
time careers. They encouraged one another to see possibilities for
themselves. As a woman in one of the focus groups said emphatically,
"We are our own role models." Postcareer but future-oriented, they
were ready to step up and make a place for themselves, individually
and collectively.

Women were energized and forthcoming when they found others
with whom they could establish common ground. Building on that
common ground, they described being ready and eager to get
involved, to take up a cause, and to be a force for change. For one
woman, the drive to find common ground was a personal commitment
that extended to her work with young people when she talked with
them about the destructiveness of hate. She connected this to her own
experiences as an immigrant whose father fought to get to America:

> Virtually everyone feels they are different. In my case, not knowing the
> language, living in a housing project, being smart, all made me feel dif-
> ferent. How do we help people see how much more alike than different
> we are?

For her, the key was "letting people be who they are." Her commitment to helping young people understand what they share, while valuing their diversity, was an enormous lesson for others.

SHARED VALUES AS A DRIVER FOR CHANGE

Values often pointed to as the bedrock of the Baby Boomer generation supported the women of Cohort 25 throughout their careers.
These values included a commitment to hard work, independence,
and high personal standards. Other values instilled by their families
often played a role in their careers: values of being generous toward
and supportive of others and having compassion and empathy. The
women themselves—as children of immigrants, as women of color,
as working mothers, as gay women, as pioneers in their professional
fields—brought experiences and perspectives to the workplace that
enriched their careers and helped them understand how to improve
the workplace for others.

As we learned from their stories, many women in Cohort 25 experienced discrimination or exclusion before laws and policies were
enacted to protect all workers. The women not only benefited from
these changes, but in several instances, they were also directly
involved in helping secure rights for themselves and others. When
the women of Cohort 25 helped create policies and negotiate for
change, their values and personal commitments to equity, justice, and
fair treatment for all were critical. These attributes were no less critical
when the women left their careers. Still energetic and empowered by a
strong social consciousness, they were prepared to become a positive
force for change. The women had internalized the fundamental importance of these protections, and they brought a firm, unequivocal commitment to diversity and equality to their postcareer lives. Working
to secure positions for people of color on corporate boards and finding
new ways to create an inclusive and affirming community for LGBT
people in nursing homes, health-care practices, and faith communities
were just two examples of the advocacy work women had taken on
after leaving their professional careers.

COMMITTED TO ACTIVE ENGAGEMENT

The goal that seemed most universally shared by the women of
Cohort 25 was that of staying connected. When women talked about
their commitment to working with others after their retirement, what
they often described was a kind of entrepreneurial engagement. They
became involved with an organization or a project, immersed themselves in a specific activity, and, when its goals had been met, they
might move on. Their accomplishments were project based. They were
no longer building a career but digging in, giving of their time and

expertise, with the recognition that they were free to move on, to try new things and experiment. They had the flexibility to put their energies where they felt they were needed, drawing on the best of their professional experiences and helping others without necessarily making a permanent, long-term commitment.

Coming from a demanding higher education environment where she was often assigned new, high-stakes projects, one woman placed a premium on managing her time and being selective after her retirement. She wanted to stay involved, especially when it came to working on "things to feed brain and spirit," but she was firm about setting boundaries: "I don't want to overcommit. I want unique opportunities, not a part-time job."

There were many places where women's engagement meant consciously working across generations. One woman was a consultant working with an expanding, family-owned company, where she was helping to develop leadership for a new era; another took on part-time projects helping young entrepreneurs get their businesses off the ground; and several were mentoring young women professionals. In every case, they were marshaling the skills and insights from their careers and passing them on in ways that would nurture and guide up-and-coming professionals. They might not have referred to themselves as "role models," but they were actively demonstrating what it meant to be a professional and bringing a range of strengths to each project: enthusiasm, hard work, creativity, and respect. Two women had made a commitment to share their expertise and counsel with young people. One stated, "I am volunteering with World Affairs Council, where I am on the board. I do a lot with the organization, developing community awareness of global issues, especially with high school and college students." Reaching across generations can involve working with institutions as well as individuals. She went on to say that in her work to develop awareness of global issues, she was especially involved in developing relationships with local colleges and universities. Another woman described using her expertise to help the next generation, noting, "I get a great deal of pleasure out of people; big pleasure out of helping young people who want to change careers."

The interest in cross-generational involvement did not flow only in the direction of passing knowledge on to younger people. Baby Boomer women were also looking more closely at the generation ahead of them, observing and learning. A writer and arts organization consultant said, "I've always been a person who gives a lot of thought about what's next . . . I kinda always know what's going to come next. I pay a lot of attention to how my friends in their eighties and nineties stay active in the world."

MAINTAINING PHYSICAL AND MENTAL HEALTH: PRAGMATIC AND PROACTIVE

We cannot talk about being future-oriented without paying attention to how women had prepared themselves for the inevitability of illness, either their own or that of a loved one. In the year after we first interviewed the women of Cohort 25, some of them dealt with serious health problems. They had joint replacements, cancer surgery, and cataract surgery. One answered our follow-up query, "What have you been doing?" by saying she had signed up for Medicare and reconfigured her will and estate plan. Another spoke of trying hard to keep in shape. She added that she had confronted something that had been of great concern to her. To dispel her fears that she might have been experiencing memory loss, she underwent seven hours of testing. "It was scary but reassuring. I wanted to clear it up, so I had one less thing to worry or distract me. Now, I don't worry any more, and because of that, my memory is better."

Women gathered great strength in dealing with concerns about their health and recognizing that bad things could and probably would happen to them and to their loved ones. They were realistic and quick to find the humor in getting older.

Speaking about a friend, one woman said, "I think I'm *her* age, and she's fifty-four. But I'm seventy!" And another, whose mother suddenly had to move into an assisted living facility in another community, found the humor to acknowledge how dramatic this change had been for *both* of them: "I still joke with my mother, 'Thank you for showing me what I have to look forward to.' "

After having been her mother's sole caretaker, she felt this move as both a relief and a loss. Her best friend had also passed away a year earlier. "Combined with my mother's moving, it took me some time to realize there was a big hole there. Well, that's life," she said. "We need to stay in the moment and love it." We have seen this resilience before, the clear-eyed, sometimes rueful, admission that things can go wrong and we need to adapt.

EMBRACING TECHNOLOGY

Apprehension that they could fall behind in critical areas of technology was expressed by some of the women as a very real concern, but in fact, their use of technology after their careers seemed to be robust and forward looking. Getting past the initial concern and having the confidence to continue to ask questions and learn about technology were actually very consistent with how they had described their interactions with technology during their careers.

Many women recalled playing a critical role in bringing technological innovation to their workplaces. They also remembered how excited they were by the potential they saw in that innovation. These comments came from several individuals who worked across a spectrum of professions, including health care, education, and publishing: "When technology went digital, I changed with it"; "When the Internet exploded, I took over as assistant superintendent for technology"; "I worked beyond the job scope and developed creative solutions, especially in the technology arena where everything was a learning curve"; "One of my most fulfilling periods was learning technology as it was evolving"; and "I helped establish technology in the hospital environment."

With more, faster, and smaller devices available each day, technology will be ubiquitous in everyone's postcareer lives. Women in Cohort 25—some retired for a number of years—were using technology in many ways. Just a few examples included teaching online courses, publishing in online journals, digitizing historical records, and conducting sophisticated stock market analyses. The women's level of engagement with and interest in contemporary technology echoed the excitement they described at bringing technology into their working lives a few decades earlier.

Social media, especially, in its many forms, was playing a significant role in women's lives after their careers. Social media had made it easier for them to stay connected, to find and arrange to meet with others with whom they had shared interests, and to create a platform for their own views. The women of Cohort 25 were learning more every day about how to make use of social media, whether they were developing a new networking profile, reaching out to business or consulting opportunities, or actively using social media to create an advocacy group. Once more, they had overcome their apprehensions and were figuring out how to use the system to their best advantage and bring their creative energy to technology.

STILL BREAKING NEW GROUND

Early in our research, we thought the phrase "still breaking new ground" might be an apt description of professional Baby Boomer women as they entered retirement. To test that premise, we included a question about the phrase in our survey. When we asked whether "still breaking new ground" resonated with them personally, the majority of the women answered yes. Some connected the sense of promise and challenge implicit in the phrase to their own lives, with comments such as these from a teacher and a journalist, both retired: "I hope to always stay current or ahead of the game no matter how old I am. I would always look for new and interesting opportunities" and "It resonates with me as it pertains to the desire to seek new professional development, new means of expression and fulfillment, and to impact society and the world."

Two other women spoke for others when they saw it as a rallying cry for their move into the future: "It validates what we have done. It shows we have more to do, and that we are counting on ourselves to do it. It's an opportunity for self-expression. We can't stop working on it" and "We continue to contribute in meaningful ways, and we want to help others to do so."

Most striking, however, was this powerful statement of purpose from a lawyer whose career had extended well beyond the practice of law. Her words reflected the leadership, resolve, and strength of Cohort 25: "We have been and will continue to be leaders. We are open to adventures and can make anything happen we set our minds to; there is collective strength; we are willing to address and confront the most important issues."

From follow-up comments, made one year after their interviews, it was clear that the women in Cohort 25 continued to see themselves as contributors in an active, ongoing process of change. They often made explicit connections between their participation in this project and their personal experiences. Their comments reinforced the importance of talking with others, listening to others, and taking time to think and be reflective. Among the things the women in Cohort 25 shared was their willingness to be both introspective *and* active. They were energized by the recognition that they could change ideas about retirement, and they were assessing their lives and what mattered to them as they entered the next stage.

What emerged most convincingly from our research was the realization that this representative group of First Wave Baby Boomer women was not finished. They had the energy, the desire, and the creativity to continue to make change. They had spent their adult lives following career paths that had often been closed to women, and they were prepared to make changes again. This time they were ready to energize popular thinking about the postcareer years, focusing on the future and celebrating what they were capable of, what they were interested in, and how much they had to give back and pass on to others. This woman could easily have been speaking for all the women in Cohort 25: "There's a big, next chapter. I don't think I'm done."

Afterword

WHEN THE WORD JUST DOESN'T FIT

Why was it so hard for the women in Cohort 25 to answer the question "What is your professional status?"

Were they leaving their careers?

Yes, but perhaps not entirely.

Were they modifying their working lives to include more flexibility, more variety?

Yes.

Were they happy to leave some aspects of their professional lives behind? Happy to be able to pick and choose where and how they would continue working?

Yes, yes.

Did they recognize and appreciate the freedom in these choices?

Yes, absolutely.

Were they retiring? Retired?

Well, those were harder questions.

When we first met the women of Cohort 25, their work status ranged from fully employed in their professions to fully retired, with several individual variations along that continuum. If they were still working, they were apprehensive about approaching *retirement*, and if they had already moved on from their full-time careers, they were careful to point out why the word "retired" was, at best, only of limited use in describing their lives. We shared their apprehensions. Although we had both left our full-time careers by the time we started this project, we were each looking for the language that we felt described who we were and how we were living our lives. We were trying to describe ourselves in spite of the word "retired."

A LABEL FROM ANOTHER TIME

"Retire"—the word itself shapes expectations and behavior in several ways, as we learned when talking with the women of Cohort 25. People identified as *retired* may chafe against the unfounded assumptions of others. Even if they are enjoying a more relaxed lifestyle, retirees do not want to be seen as being out of touch personally or professionally. Many retirees continue to have very full schedules, often including paid work or consulting. They find it difficult to respond to well-meaning friends or former coworkers who refer longingly to "how nice it must be" to be retired. Women in Cohort 25 were especially uneasy with characterizations of retirement that sounded falsely celebratory while they were busy living their lives and anticipating the future with the same level of drive and confidence they had known all along. They were not looking for high-fives of encouragement any more than they wished to be called "ma'am" or "dear."

The reality is that the word "retire" is an inherited cultural and linguistic shorthand. When it is used to refer collectively and indiscriminately to the lives of millions of people, it can easily feel like a mismatch between language and reality. As often happens with attempts to label groups of people, the word "retired" reduces individual differences to an uneasy common denominator.

The concept of withdrawing to a well-earned period of rest has been embedded in the word "retire" for over three hundred years. With etymological roots in *re* and *tirer*, literally, "to withdraw," the word "retire" carries within it a history that emphasizes the retreat from activity to leisure. Although earlier uses of the word are documented from the mid-1500s, by the time Samuel Pepys was writing in 1667, "retire" had definitely taken on the meaning of "give[ing] up one's business or occupation in order to enjoy more leisure or freedom (especially after having made a competence or earned a pension)."[1]

A term derived from the idea of "retreating or withdrawing" simply does not do justice to how people are living after their careers today. Their lives could more appropriately be described as actively engaging, *not* retreating; reaching out, *not* withdrawing. When Baby Boomers object to the word "retire," they are trying to resist becoming hostage to a word whose connotations deny the expansiveness, engagement, and energy that characterize their lives. What they want instead is to level the playing field once more, to be valued and accepted forthrightly for the people they are, what they have accomplished, and what they have to give.

As a group, Baby Boomers cannot easily fit their experiences into norms that were established at a very different time, when there were very different expectations for life after the age of sixty-five. According to numbers provided by the Social Security Administration website, the average projected life expectancy for individuals who reach age sixty-five has increased about seven years over what it was for both men and women in 1940,[2] but that number alone does not reflect the exponential increase in opportunities enjoyed by today's sixty-five-year-olds. Nor does it reflect their energy and expectations. They are physically healthy, mentally acute, and armed with actuarial projections for a life expectancy of 86.6 years for women and 84.3 years for men. Yet, despite their vigor, retirees today still face stereotypes perpetuated by the earlier model of life in retirement, when the years after age sixty-five were considered "old" and when many individuals were content to stop working and enjoy their remaining years without looking back.

FIND A NEW LABEL?

We are not the first to realize how much the word "retirement" shortchanges those who are leaving their full-time careers but who are *not* planning to withdraw. In fact, *retiring* is the last thing on their minds! The lessons from the women of Cohort 25 were explicit in demonstrating how life in retirement can be active and forward-looking. That is hardly the same sense of what it meant to *retire* in seventeenth-century England.

Just as other words have fallen from use as the culture has changed,[3] "retire," too, could be sloughed off and replaced by a term that accurately reflects this stage of life as robust, mindful, and giving. In fact, much has been written about finding alternatives to the word, and many artists, sociologists, and psychologists are examining how what we think of as "retirement"—both the *action* of leaving a career and the *social status* that follows—is changing and will continue to change.

Here are just a few of the terms that have been used to describe the new stage Baby Boomers are entering after leaving their full-time careers. Many of them underscore the idea of a new beginning, a separate, discrete *stage of life* in later adulthood: "encore," "second act," "third act," "next act," "life 2.5," "unretirement," and "renewment." Other newly coined terms emphasize the *process* a person goes through: "retooling," "reimagining," and "rebooting."

Although these words and phrases may accurately capture the sense of reinvention people have described, we are beginning to think that finding a new term is not the most important challenge we face when describing life after a full-time career.

BETTER YET, SHIFT THE FOCUS

We suggest turning attention away from the shortcomings of the word "retire" and focusing instead on how people are actually living their lives. Considering the larger group of Baby Boomer professional women of which Cohort 25 was a very small sample, let's look at how these women, as a whole, are changing the culture again. Just as they entered the workplace loaded with confidence and ambition, they are entering retirement with decades of accumulated professional experience. During their careers, they provided real-time examples of what women were capable of. They changed the workplace in permanent ways so that young women really could see themselves in any profession to which they aspired. What are they doing now? How are they using their strengths to give new meaning to retirement?

If we think of the life stage labeled *retirement* as a continuation of our professional lives, we shift the focus and begin to accept retirement as a new period of engagement, with its own goals and aspirations. Retired people are less busy in certain ways but still fully engaged. The women of Cohort 25 provided several good examples. They might have been placing less emphasis on external career demands in order to pay attention to and nurture personal qualities in themselves and others. At the same time, they were committed to staying involved, perhaps still earning a salary. They were working with others, giving back to their communities, looking for meaningful ways to stay connected.

The lives of Cohort 25 and other Baby Boomers demonstrate that we need not so much a new name or label but a *new understanding* of the potential of our later years. If we take the emphasis off the word "retirement" and look instead at what is happening after people's full-time careers, we realize it is less important to label a brand-new "stage" than it is to see this period as a continuation and improvement of the lives they have lived.

By paying attention and describing candidly what this period is really like, we can look carefully at the deepening sense of self and the new commitment to engagement that characterize individuals who are age sixty and older. Their professional lives made an impact on others; their lives in retirement will shape others' impressions in ways that a new label cannot capture.

There is no doubt that for countless Baby Boomers, and most assuredly for the generations that follow us, life in our later decades is going to be different from what it was for our parents and grandparents. In her TED Talk, "Life's Third Act," Jane Fonda spoke eloquently about how the thirty-four years' greater life expectancy that we have gained since our *great-grandparents'* generation allows us the opportunity to live our lives, especially our later years, with greater personal focus. She emphasized, especially through the metaphor of aging as a staircase that we ascend in an upward evolution, that this period of our lives allows us time to reflect on our past experiences "and that helps us become whole, brings wisdom and authenticity."[4] The idea that we continue to grow, to become wiser and better versions of ourselves, helps us see this time of life as an important, transformative period that defies any easy labels.

GREATER FLEXIBILITY AND AUTONOMY

A woman in Cohort 25 captured the conundrum at the heart of the word "retire" very simply: "I'm not retired in the usual sense. I am continuing to work."

Much as millennials have changed the concept of work—by working from home, not making career-long commitments to a single profession or institution, and advocating for the flexibility to take care of family and health matters—so too, Baby Boomers facing the traditional age of retirement are finding ways to renegotiate what it means to "keep working." Many of the changes they are seeking are similar to those of the millennials, with the desire for flexibility being the most important.

As a representative sample of First Wave Baby Boomers, the women in Cohort 25 wanted to be seen as moving into the future with many of the same traits that helped them thrive during their careers. They were also open to exploring how a new sense of identity and commitment to helping others could reinvigorate their role in the workplace, regardless of where and how they were working. They were not fighting for the right to continue to have a competitive career in the workforce. Instead, they were looking to be acknowledged as viable participants in the workforce, valued for their ideas and insights. One woman with extensive experience as a hospital administrator and corporate operations professional said during her interview, "I would like to see in the workplace a new, accepted stage of employment for older workers, where their knowledge and experience are considered valuable assets to a company's success and bottom-line profits."

BABY BOOMER WOMEN CHANGING THE CULTURE
FROM WITHIN, AGAIN

Once again, the larger group of Baby Boomer professional women, of which Cohort 25 is a sample, will be the first to challenge an old expectation; this time, it is the expectation about what it means to be retired. These women didn't struggle to find a new name for the workplace during their careers, but by their presence and contributions, they remade it. As they step out of their full-time careers, they are bringing an entirely new, active cohort into the culture of retirement. This generation will be the first to challenge the assumptions about retirement *in such large numbers.* And once again, Baby Boomer women are entering a new stage of their lives at a critical moment of cultural change, just as they entered their careers at a transformative period in history, thirty to forty years ago.

The women of Cohort 25 said it plainly: they were not going to slip quietly into the sunset. Through their presence and actions, they were prepared to make change again. Their influence in expanding the meaning of retirement reflected the reality of a new era. With many productive years ahead of them, they would continue to radically remake what it meant to be retired for decades to come.

Labels are not what matters. We should pay attention instead to the actions and voices of Baby Boomer women, as represented by Cohort 25. These women are shifting to a new way of working. They are approaching the years after their full-time careers with expectations much like those of their younger counterparts, seeking a balance of work, personal life, family, and friends and placing a very high premium on flexibility.

No matter what it is called, the retirement of Baby Boomer professional women will look different from what we thought of as retirement in the past. They changed the workplace, and they will surely change what comes next.

NOTES

1. *The Compact Edition of the Oxford English Dictionary,* s.v. "retire."
2. When monthly benefits started in 1940, the average remaining life expectancy for those surviving to sixty-five was 12.7 years for men (or age 77.7) and 14.7 years for women (or age 79.7). "Social Security History," U.S. Social Security Administration, accessed March 4, 2017, https://www.ssa. gov/history/lifeexpect.html.Today, a man reaching age 65 can expect to live, on average, until age 84.3. A woman turning age 65 today can expect to live, on average, until age 86.6. "Calculators: Life Expectancy," U.S. Social

Security Administration, accessed March 4, 2017, https://www.ssa.gov/planners/lifeexpectancy.html.

3. Many other words once used to refer to women or women's work, such as "spinster," "beldam," "damsel," and "distaff," have dropped out of popular usage. Their use today is clearly recognized as archaic or possibly ironic.

4. Jane Fonda, "Life's Third Act." Filmed December 2011. TED video, 11:20. Posted January 2012, https://www.ted.com/talks/jane_fonda_life_s_third_act. This talk was among many recommendations we received from Cohort 25 members for materials they had found personally exciting and helpful in their own career transitions. We did not specifically ask the group for recommendations, but we welcomed this suggestion as well as others that came our way, knowing the women in Cohort 25 are avid consumers of many forms of media. One woman was approaching her fiftieth book of the year the last time we spoke with her, and another said she was constantly "power reading." Here are a few of the books they mentioned as being helpful:Mihaly Csikszentmihalyi, *Flow: The Psychology of Optimal Experience* (New York: Harper & Row, 1990).Deborah M. Kolb, Judith Williams, and Carol Frohlinger, *Her Place at the Table: A Woman's Guide to Negotiating Five Key Challenges to Leadership Success* (San Francisco, CA: Jossey-Bass, 2004). Adam Grant, *Give and Take: Why Helping Others Drives Our Success* (New York: Viking, 2013).One person also mentioned Gail Sheehy's classic work, *Passages: Predictable Crises of Adult Life* (New York: E.P. Dutton, 1974), specifically because, as she said, "Everyone I know is in the midst of change."

Bibliography

Baird-Krul, Carol, and Enise Olding. *Transition to Retirement: The Uncharted Course*. Gabriola, BC: Pacific Edge, 2006.

Bateson, Mary Catherine. *Composing a Life*. New York: Grove Press, 1989.

Bateson, Mary Catherine. *Composing a Further Life: The Age of Active Wisdom*. New York: Knopf, 2010.

Boston Women's Health Book Collective. *Our Bodies, Ourselves: A Book by and for Women*. New York: Simon & Schuster, 1973.

Bratter, Bernice, and Helen Dennis. *Project Renewment*. New York: Scribner, 2008.

Collins, Gail. *When Everything Changed: The Amazing Journey of American Women from 1960 to the Present*. New York: Little, Brown, 2009.

Croker, Richard. *The Boomer Century 1946–2046*. New York: Springboard Press, 2007.

Eliot, T. S. *The Complete Poems and Plays 1909–1950*. New York: Harcourt, Brace & World, 1934.

Farley, Reynolds. *The New American Reality: Who We Are, How We Got Here, Where Are We Going*. New York: Russell Sage Foundation, 1996.

Fideler, Elizabeth F. *Women Still at Work: Professionals over Sixty and on the Job*. Lanham, MD: Rowman & Littlefield, 2012.

Hannon, Kerry. *Great Jobs for Everyone 50+*. Hoboken, NJ: John Wiley, 2012.

Herr, Lois Kathryn. *Women, Power, and AT&T: Winning Rights in the Workplace*. Boston: Northeastern University Press, 2003.

Pauley, Jane. *Your Life Calling: Reimagining the Rest of Your Life*. New York: Simon & Schuster, 2014.

Sheehy, Gail. *New Passages: Mapping Your Life across Time.* New York: Random House, 1995.

Sheehy, Gail. *Passages: Predictable Crises of Adult Life.* New York: E.P. Dutton, 1974.

Sherr, Lynn. *Sally Ride: America's First Woman in Space.* New York: Simon & Schuster, 2014.

The Transition Network and Gail Rentsch. *Smart Women Don't Retire— They Break Free.* New York: Springboard Press, 2008.

Twenge, Jean M., Elise C. Freeman, and W. Keith Campbell. "Generational Differences in Young Adults' Life Goals, Concern for Others, and Civic Orientation, 1966–2009." *Journal of Personality and Social Psychology* 102, no. 5 (2012): 1045–106.

ONLINE RESOURCES

Albernaz, Ami. "How Men and Women Retire." *Boston Globe* (Home Life), December 29, 2015. https://www.bostonglobe.com/lifestyle/2015/12/28/how-men-and-women-retire/3d2OKYDMQnHPJKRDt9gLkM/story.html.

"APA Survey Finds US Employers Unresponsive to Employee Needs: Women Feel Less Valued, Have Few Opportunities at Work." American Psychological Association, March 5, 2013. http://www.apa.org/news/press/releases/2013/03/employee-needs.aspx.

"Baby Boomers: From the Age of Aquarius to the Age of Responsibility." Pew Research Center: Social & Demographic Trends, December 8, 2005. www.pewsocialtrends.org/2005/121/08/baby-boomers-from-the-age-of-aquarius-to-the-age-of-responsibility/.

"Baby Boomers: The Gloomiest Generation." Pew Research Center: Social & Demographic Trends, June 25, 2008. www.pewsocialtrends.org/2008/06/25/baby-boomers-the-gloomiest-generation/.

"Baby Boomers." History. Accessed March 15, 2017. http://www.history.com/topics/baby-boomers.

"BBHQ Boomer Essays: Boomer Statistics." Baby Boomer Headquarters. http://www.bbhq.com/bomrstat.htm.

Block, Sandra. "8 Ways Baby-Boomers Are Reinventing Retirement." Kiplinger, May 2013. http://www.kiplinger.com/slideshow/retirement/T037-S000-8-ways-baby-boomers-are-reinventing-retirement/index.html.

Brandon, Emily. "10 Ways Baby Boomers Will Reinvent Retirement." US News and World Report, February 16, 2010. http://money.usnews.com/money/retirement/articles/2010/02/16/10-ways-baby-boomers-will-reinvent-retirement.

"Calculators: Life Expectancy." U.S. Social Security Administration. Accessed March 4, 2017. https://www.ssa.gov/planners/lifeexpectancy.html.

"The Civil Rights Act of 1964: A Long Struggle for Freedom." Library of Congress. Accessed March 28, 2017. https://www.loc.gov/exhibits/civil-rights-act/civil-rights-act-of-1964.html.

Cook, Nancy. "Will Baby Boomers Change the Meaning of Retirement?" *Atlantic*, June 28, 2015. https://www.theatlantic.com/business/archive/2015/06/baby-boomersretirement/396950/.

Coontz, Stephanie. "The M.R.S. and Ph.D." *New York Times* (Sunday Review: Opinion), February 11, 2012. http://www.nytimes.com/2012/02/12/opinion/sunday/marriage-suits-educated-women.html?_r=0.

Eisenberg, Richard. "The Good News about Women Working after 60." nextavenue, July 20, 2012. http://www.nextavenue.org/good-news-about-women-working-after-60/.

Fonda, Jane. "Life's Third Act." Filmed December 2011. TED video, 11:20. Posted January 2012. https://www.ted.com/talks/jane_fonda_life_s_third_act.

Imbornoni, Ann-Marie. "Women's Rights Movement in the U.S." Infoplease. Accessed March 8, 2017. http://www.infoplease.com/spot/womenstimeline2.html.

"Important Supreme Court Cases for Civil Rights." The Leadership Conference. Accessed March 8, 2017. http://www.civilrights.org/judiciary/supreme-court/key-cases.html.

Olauson, Anders. "Changing the Culture of Retirement." BlackRock, December 14, 2016. https://www.blackrock.com/corporate/en-gb/insights/blackrock-retirement-institute/workforce-and-economics/changing-the-culture-of-retirement/.

Pathe, Simone. "Why Some Women Try to Have It All: New Research on 'Like Mother, Like Daughter.'" *PBS Newshour*, November 20, 2013. http://www.pbs.org/newshour/making-sense/why-some-women-try-to-have-it/.

"Social Security History." U.S. Social Security Administration. Accessed March 4, 2017. https://www.ssa.gov/history/lifeexpect.html.

Thomas, Marlo. "Free to Be ... You and Me—Forty Years Later." *Huffington Post* (blog), November 30, 2012, updated January 30, 2013. http://www.huffingtonpost.com/marlo-thomas/free-to-be-40-years-later_b_2206066.html.

Turner, Natasha. "10 Things That American Women Could Not Do before the 1970s." *Ms. Magazine* (blog), May 28, 2013. http://msmagazine.com/blog/2013/05/28/10-things-that-american-women-could-not-do-before-the-1970s/.

ABOUT THE AUTHORS

ANNE C. COON is professor emerita at Rochester Institute of Technology (RIT) in Rochester, New York. She is the author of many academic and general interest books and articles and has often collaborated across traditional academic disciplines. Her books include *Hear Me Patiently: The Reform Speeches of Amelia Jenks Bloomer* (Greenwood Publishing) and the coauthored *Discovering Patterns in Mathematics and Poetry* (Editions Rodopi) as well as books of poetry and joint creative projects with artists and photographers. She earned a PhD in English literature from the State University of New York at Buffalo and served on the faculty of RIT for twenty-eight years, retiring as professor of English and senior associate dean in the College of Liberal Arts.

JUDITH ANN FEUERHERM's career spans forty years of diverse experience. Most currently she was the practice leader for the northeastern U.S. career management services of an international company, Right Management. In that role she led a team of consultants ensuring excellence of coaching for individuals and delivery of coaching services to individuals and groups impacted by large corporate downsizings. Her focus is primarily in looking to the future as a guide in coaching individuals and guiding them to realize and match assets to areas of interest to optimize their personal and professional goals. She has an MA in journalism from Temple University and a BFA from Empire State College (SUNY).